# What Others Are Saying...

"A wonderful financial tutorial which toggles nicely between a roller coaster metaphor and some cold, hard facts. Everyone should take the Money Ride."

—Joseph Engelberg, Ph.D.
Assistant Professor of Finance
University of North Carolina

"A compelling explanation of how, throughout life, one can make better decisions about money... Without insulting our intelligence he makes certain that even the most elementary issues are understood... A most enjoyable and illuminating ride!"

—Richard Farson, author, psychologist
President, Western Behavioral Sciences Institute

"As economic cycles come and go this book will hold up as a primer for anyone who wants to understand the basics of wealth accumulation and preservation. *The Money Ride* enhances money intelligence and money behavior."

—Vaughn Woods, CFP, MBA

"Much more than a how-to-balance-a-checkbook book, *The Money Ride* provides an excellent road map for developing a clear perspective on the key factors of life including, but not limited to, money."

—Ed Blitz, CPA, author
*The 10% Solution-Your Key to Financial Security*

# The
# Money
# Ride

## A Passenger's Guide to Money & Wealth

### William K. Busch

illustrations by Dennis L. Busch

2010
KALA PUBLISHING
LA JOLLA, CALIFORNIA

ISBN 978-0-9826393-0-6

Type design by Studio E Books, Santa Barbara, Calif.
www.studio-e-books.com

Published by Kala Publishing
Post Office Box 1152
La Jolla, CA 92038
www.moneyride.com

## Acknowledgments

Many people contributed to this book, but two people in particular contributed to its early stages of development: Cathy Kijak-Tyre and David Jones. Over the past ten years, both have given me the opportunity to work with their students to develop and refine the Money Ride concepts and test the teaching approach.

I have not attempted to cite in the text all of the sources consulted in writing this book. To do so would require more pages than would be practical. The list would include government departments, periodicals, colleagues and experts in the fields of economics, finance, real estate, investing and psychology.

There are, however, a few individuals who deserve special mention because their insights, values and life examples have influenced and inspired my thoughts on money and wealth: Vaughn Woods, George Fermanian, Michael Phillips and Victor Canto.

Many thanks to Gordon Burgett for his expert guidance and encouragement in the early stages of this project. The advice and support in the final stages from Vincent D'Addona and Vincent Carissimi were critical to completing this book.

Very special thanks to Bill Butler whose patience and help with writing and editing was vital, Dennis Busch for illustrating, Eric Larson for the book design and Doug Burgett for the cover design.

Finally, most important of all…to Diane, Josef and Julia—without your love, support and encouragement, *The Money Ride* would still just be an idea.

# Contents

Introduction

**1. The Ride / 13**
Welcome!
Making the Most of Your Turn

**2. The Rules / 19**
The Grabbing Rules
Your Work I.Q.
Your Money I.Q.

**3. Money Dynamics / 27**
The Uses of Money
Meet Your Fellow Passengers
The Mechanics of Money
PAW and MAW
Money Decay

**4. Stashing Your Cash / 43**
The Opportunity Vest
Vest Dynamics

**5. The Spend Pocket / 49**
PAW at Work
Your Friend Bud
Budget = $D^2$
Building Your Budget
Sample Monthly Budget

**6. The Save Pocket / 63**
Here Comes MAW
Save = Safe
How Much?
How Soon/How Long?
Where?

**7. The Invest Pocket / 75**
> MAW Goes to Work
> Wealth
> Invest = Risk
> The Three Levels of Risk
> Invest = Reward
> Invest = Growth
> Invest = Income
> Mechanics of Investing
> How Much?
> How Soon/How Long?
> Where?
> Business Ownership
> Stocks
> Bonds
> Mutual Funds
> Real Estate
> OPM

**8. The Protect Pocket / 105**
> Expect the Unexpected
> Health, Income, Property & Life
> Risk Transfer
> Cost Sharing
> Full Replacement Value

**9. The Borrow Pocket / 115**
> Borrowing: From $D^2$ to $-S^2$
> OPM Mechanics
> Good Debt & Bad Debt
> Your Borrowing Score

**10. Time to Buckle Up! / 127**

**Glossary of Money Ride Terms / 129**

# The
# Money
# Ride

# Introduction

Have you ever been to an amusement park? If you have, did you find the Money Ride? If you didn't, you missed the most amazing ride of them all! But don't feel bad, because you're not the only one.

The Money Ride is hard to find, by design. It isn't noisy and flashy like the other rides. It's just a giant, plain, box-looking building with an entrance marked "$TART" at one side and an exit marked "FINI$H" at the other side.

It's what's inside the Money Ride that makes it the most exciting, scariest and longest ride in the park!

Inside, there's a wind tunnel containing a huge roller coaster with trillions of dollar bills swirling all around you. The fantastic thing about the Money Ride is that from the time you enter until you exit *you get to use and enjoy all the money you grab!*

This book shows you how you can get on the Money Ride and make the most of your trip. As you read these pages, you will learn how to effectively manage and grow your money to create the life you want to live. The valuable, easy-to-remember money tools and tips will help you take advantage of every up, down, twist and turn.

You will not be alone on your Money Ride adventure. Along the way, you will meet some of your fellow passengers and learn from their good and bad money decisions. Observing their choices will help you create and sustain sound money habits that will enable you to live a happier, more prosperous life. So, buckle up and get ready to enjoy the Money Ride—it's the ride of a lifetime and we are all on it!

# 1. The Ride

## Welcome!

Welcome to the Money Ride! This book is both your admission ticket to get you on the ride and your passenger guide for making your turn on the ride an unforgettable adventure.

As you wait in line, anxious for your turn to begin, you can only imagine what it's going to be like. How wild and radical can the roller coaster ride be? And what about all that money swirling about—all for the taking? You're getting more and more excited and anxious as you visualize all the money you're going to grab and all the stuff you're going to be able to buy.

The line shuffles forward and soon you can hear the shouting, screaming and laughter as the people ahead of you disappear behind the big door labeled "$TART."

While you wait, you're frantically thumbing the pages of your passenger guide searching for every advantage you can give yourself once you get inside. The more you read the more you begin to realize that this concept of "use and enjoy all the money you grab" probably won't be as easy as it sounds—and you're right.

Like most of the rides at the amusement park, the Money Ride has rules that you must follow. Unlike the other rides, it's not about how old you are, how big you are or even about keeping your arms inside the car.

On the Money Ride the rules determine how much money you will be able to grab—these are called the Grabbing Rules. We will cover these rules shortly, but first we're going to talk about how you can make the most of your turn on the Money Ride.

## Making the Most of Your Turn

The Money Ride is called "The Ride of a Lifetime" because your pursuit of financial success is a lifelong adventure.

Your passenger guide provides you with information on the basic principles of money. Because the basic principles of money and wealth do not change, they serve as a consistent basis and guide for making smart money decisions and achieving financial success.

Each passenger on the Money Ride has their own personal definition of what it means to be financially successful. Their definitions are unique, but they all describe a particular quality of life.

Your definition describes what your life will feel like once you have achieved financial success in terms of happiness, health, security, and freedom. This guide will help you to develop the money skills required to create the money and wealth you will need to live that life.

Regardless of how you define financial success, your ultimate success will be determined by what you know about money and how you behave with money.

The definition of financial success will vary from passenger to passenger on the Money Ride, but the process for achieving financial success is the same for everyone. It is a process of long-term financial progress based on money knowledge and behavior.

Because knowledge and behavior are so important, the first step to achieving financial success consists of creating sound money habits. This involves focusing your money behavior according to the simple, time-tested principles of money explained in this guide.

The key is to not just read the money principles, tips and tools in this guide, but to use them to guide your money behavior through sound money habits.

Consistent sound money habits will enable you to become financially self-reliant. Financial self-reliance is the first stage of the achieving financial success. It is the key to financial freedom and prosperity, because if you don't control your money, your money will control you. Passengers who are financially self-reliant have much more fun and opportunity on the Money Ride!

So, the sooner you begin to develop sound money habits, the sooner you will begin to reap the full rewards of your adventure on the Money Ride.

 **Passenger Tips & Tools #1**

### Five Steps to Creating Sound Money Habits

1. Think about how your life could be different if you did a better job of controlling your money ...happiness, freedom, security, etc. These are your rewards for creating sound money habits...why it's important to you.

2. Focus on creating one new habit at a time.

3. On the top half of 3x5 note card, describe how good it feels that you are in control of your money...in the present tense as though you are already there. For example use positive statements like "I'm proud of myself for how carefully I manage my money."

4. On the bottom half of the card now describe the habit your are going to work on...again in the present tense as though you're already doing it. Describe it is a specific action like, "I keep track of the money I earn and spend."

5. Display the 3x5 card where you will see it every night and morning. EVERY DAY!!!...twice each day, (morning and night) read the card, repeating AT LEAST TEN TIMES...the reward and the habit to yourself verbally and mentally.

Repeat the exercise twice each day until the new habit becomes part of your normal thought process, stimulating a positive mental reminder every time you make a choice with your money.

# 2. The Rules

## The Grabbing Rules

From the time you enter through the $tart door to the time you exit through the Fini$h door you get to use and enjoy all the money you grab—"Grabbing Dollars." How much you grab will depend upon these rules.

1. **If you don't graduate from high school.** You must keep your hands in your pockets and use only your teeth, elbows and knees to grab dollars.

2. **If you graduate from high school.** You are allowed to take your hands out of your pockets to grab more dollars.

3. **If you earn an AA degree or learn a marketable skill/trade.** You are given a small butterfly net to grab more dollars.

4. **If you earn a BA/BS degree.** You are given a medium-size butterfly net to grab still more dollars.

5. **If you earn a MA/MS degree.** You are given a large butterfly net to grab still more dollars.

6. **If you earn a PhD, MD or JD.** You are given a giant butterfly net to grab still more dollars.

7. **If you are a business owner.** You are given a giant butterfly net. You're also allowed to bring your employees on the ride with you and you get a bonus dollar for every dollar your employees grab.

As you study these Grabbing Rules you can see a connection between your opportunity to grab dollars and your level of formal education. It's as if you actually get paid to go to school.

"Can't be true," you say? Well it is true and there is data to prove it. Each year, the government keeps track of what everybody in the U.S. earns and spends…how they earn it and how they spend it.

The government data examine earning and spending in different ways, looking for trends and connections between the two. One of the connections is the relationship between a person's education level and their earnings. So, let's look at what the data tells us about the connection between earnings and education.

### U.S. Census Bureau
### 2007 American Community Survey
### Median Earnings by Educational Attainment

| Education Level | Annual Wages | Career Total[1] | Increase[2] |
|---|---|---|---|
| HS Dropout | $18,402 | $736,080 | |
| HS Diploma | $26,827 | $1,073,080 | $337,000 |
| AA Degree | $34,041 | $1,361,640 | $288,560 |
| BA/BS Degree | $48,013 | $1,920,520 | $588,880 |
| MA/PhD/JD/MD | $64,078 | $2,563,120 | $642,600 |

[1] Career time span, 40 years
[2] Earnings increase over prior education level

Now that you've seen the data supporting the connection between education and income, let's go back to the question, Do you actually get paid to go to school?

We essentially get paid for the time we are in school the same way that professional athletes and CEOs of large corporations receive some of their pay…it's called *"deferred income."*

Deferred income is pay you receive at some point in the future after you have done the work according to some acceptable standard. The government data simply verifies that you really do get paid at some point in the future for every minute you spend educating yourself.

**Passenger Tips & Tools #2**

Do you know someone who is thinking about dropping out of high school or who actually has dropped out of high school? Well, if you do, go to that person and tell them you that you know someone who will pay them $300,000 if they will just hang in there and get their high school diploma.

U.S. Government data show that assuming a 40-year working career, a person with a high school diploma will earn an average of approximately $300,000 more than a high school dropout.

## Your Work I.Q.

From the government data, you can see the direct relationship between formal education and income in our society. On the Money Ride this is called your "Work I.Q."

Your Work I.Q. is all of the education, job skills and personal skills you acquire that enable you to earn an income.

Be aware that the government data are based on averages, which can be deceiving. This means that on the Money Ride, your level of formal education is not an accurate predictor of income, unless you are content to just be average. The passengers who maximize their education/income potential on the Money Ride know that you don't really get paid the big dollars for just showing up at school.

You really get paid to acquire knowledge and skills which are marketable—knowledge and skills which employers and customers need or want and will pay for. This means that your Work I.Q. is really your *work product,* consisting of your education, technical skills and personal attributes which enable you to be a productive worker.

Education and technical skills, as they relate to a particular job, are easy to define. Personal skills, on the other hand, are more general in their application and are important in all types of work. Personal skills consist of two basic aspects: people skills and work ethic.

Your people skills enable you to interact with your superiors, fellow workers and customers in a positive manner. On the Money Ride, no matter how smart or well trained you are, you will never reach your full grabbing potential without people skills.

Your work ethic defines what kind of worker you are—it is your attitude and approach to your work. The stronger your work ethic is, the more reliable and productive a worker you will be.

How much you can sell your work product for depends upon the demand for it and your competition. The better paying the job, the more competition you will face.

You will compete for jobs against your fellow passengers, initially based upon your education, technical skills and work experience. When these fail to give you a competitive advantage, your personal attributes may mean the difference. In these cases, your work ethic will help set you apart from your competition.

---

 **Passenger Tips & Tools #3**

### What kind of worker are you?

Business owners know that when it comes to hiring workers…"Good people are hard to find."

If you want to be a worker in demand, be the kind of worker you would hire if you were a business owner.

Here are three simple but important things you need to do to make the most of your value to a business:

1. Be on time
2. Do what you say you are going to do.
3. Communicate clearly in spoken and written word.

---

As a passenger, you can only optimize your grabbing opportunity if your Work I.Q. has purpose and focus. To find your purpose and focus, explore different possibilities to discover what you're interested in, what's important to you, what you like or dislike and what you're good at.

Like most passengers on the Money Ride, you will likely have many different jobs during your turn. It may take a lot of job sampling before you find the field or job that best suits you. Don't be afraid to try new job experiences—they are an important part of developing your Work I.Q.

Thanks to technology, you will have many job and career opportunities to choose from on the Money Ride. New industries emerge every year, needing educated workers with versatile skills. Be bold, conscientious, enthusiastic, determined and persistent in your pursuit.

As your Work I.Q. and productivity continue to grow, you will always be in demand. Remember that if you have purpose and focus, the more you learn…the more you earn.

**High School Diploma**
Congratulations!
This Diploma-Coupon is good for
additional lifetime earnings valued at

# $300,000

And there's more where this came from!

## Your Money I.Q.

No matter how developed your Work I.Q. is, it will only take you so far on the Money Ride.

If you really want to enjoy a successful financial life, you need to realize that your income is only the raw material of financial success.

The key to making the most of your turn on the Money Ride will be your ability to create wealth by dynamically deploying the income that you grab. This will require a type of intelligence which is different from your Work I.Q.—your "Money I.Q."

While there is a direct connection between Work I.Q. and income, there is no such connection between Work I.Q. and wealth.

The amount of wealth you acquire during your turn on the Money Ride will therefore be determined by your Money I.Q., rather than by your Work I.Q.

Your Money I.Q. consists of two basic parts:

1. Your knowledge and understanding of how money works.
2. Your ability to successfully apply that knowledge to a lifetime of money choices and decisions.

Both of these important parts are covered in the sections which follow. Keep reading and by the time your turn on the Money Ride begins, you'll have a strong foundation of money knowledge to help you make the most of the opportunities to turn your Grabbing Dollars into wealth.

# 3. Money Dynamics

## The Uses of Money

You're getting really close now! So close that you can hear the roar of the roller coaster, feel the wind escaping from under the $TART door and you can even smell the money! There's not much time, so you need to carefully read these next few pages in your passenger's guide, because it's important that you learn "Money Dynamics" before you start your turn.

Money Dynamics consist of two dynamic aspects of money which you must understand if want to make the most of your ride: the Uses of Money and the Mechanics of Money. How much success you enjoy on the Money Ride will depend on your ability to understand and apply these two dynamics through your Money I.Q.

If you understand the Uses of Money and the Mechanics of Money, your Money I.Q. will continue to grow more productive as you progress from choice to choice and decision to decision on your Money Ride adventure.

Each of the dollars that you will grab during your turn on the Money Ride will serve one or more of the following basic roles or functions of money:

1. **Medium of Exchange.** This is the first, most important and most valuable use of money—buying stuff. Money is the primary exchange commodity used for all purchases and sales. The economy originally operated on the barter system, where you traded commodities like pigs and corn for other goods and services. But since pigs and corn come in different types and sizes, it was difficult to standardize the value of units being traded. Also, it was difficult to divide pigs and corn into smaller units, making it a real challenge to make change!

    To solve the problem of standard value and divisibility,

the pigs and corn were replaced with a different trading commodity, currency—pieces of paper (dollars) with a standard value. So, when it comes to buying and selling stuff, dollars are like paper substitutes for pigs and corn.

Whether it's stuff you need or stuff you want, the ability to trade dollars for goods and services is what makes things happen on the Money Ride.

2. **Measure of Price or Value.** How much does it cost and how much is it worth? Can you afford it? Is it a fair price or good deal? On the Money Ride all of these questions are answered in dollar units.

3. **Units for Storing Wealth.** How much is all your stuff worth? In this role, the dollar is used as the measure of how much wealth you accumulate in the form of stuff called assets or property that you own. It also measures how the value of your wealth changes over time.

All your stuff is generally called "property," and "assets" are a special type of property. Assets are special because they create wealth. An asset is any property which grows in value and/or generates income.

On the Money Ride, the dollar is the measure of how much wealth you are creating and whether your wealth is growing or shrinking as you roll along.

4. **Display of Wealth.** The value of a dollar can also be used to show people how much wealth you have. It can be in the form of expensive, flashy cars, huge homes, fancy clothing and jewelry or other property which gives the impression to other passengers that you have lots of wealth.

So, now that you know the four important roles of money, how do you think and feel about each of the roles money plays? Which role do you think has the most influence over your money decisions?

How you answer these questions about money tells you something about the kind of "Money Person" you are.

What kind of Money Person are you? How do you feel about spending, saving, making and losing money? Are you a "penny pincher" or a "free spender"? Is it important to you that people know or can guess how much money you have?

You may even find yourself behaving like a different type at different times—that's okay as long as you are aware of how your thinking affects your actions. Your ability to change your thinking and behavior will enable you to establish and maintain sound money habits that will enhance your chances for financial success.

## Meet Your Fellow Passengers

Watching your fellow passengers on the Money Ride will help you with your thinking and behavior. Watching them will allow you to reflect on your own money behavior. It will help you verify through their life examples that sound money habits really do work. You are about to meet four passengers each of whom represents a type of behavior related to the use of money. You will be able to learn from seeing how they go about the business of deploying the dollars they manage to grab. Watch closely and be aware that there are many variations and degrees of these four basic behavior types.

Every passenger on the Money Ride uses money as a medium of exchange, but how they go about it differs based on their attitudes about money—how they relate to money. You will see some of yourself in them, as the Money Person they are influences their money decisions.

So, let's take a moment to meet some of the people who will be on the ride with you.

**Suzie Spender.** Like most people, Suzie likes buying stuff. To her, every dollar she grabs on the Money Ride "is meant to be spent." As soon as a dollar hits Suzie's hands the temptation to spend it grabs hold and dominates her money decisions. You will learn some important lessons from watching how Suzie handles her money.

**Franklin Frugal.** Franklin is a super shopper whose money behavior is driven by price and value. He understands the difference between price and cost and knows value when he sees it. Franklin never pays more for something than he must. He is always on the lookout for good deals and bargains. You will do well to pay attention to how Franklin makes decisions with his money.

**Sonya Stockpiler.** Having lots of money stashed away is really what drives Sonya's money decisions. She loves her units of stored value and keeps a close watch on how much money she has and where it is stockpiled. Sonya carefully watches every dollar she grabs and tries to stash as many dollars as she can in savings and investments. You will learn a lot about wealth-building habits by watching Sonya work with her money.

**Freddy Flash.** Freddy is really proud of his wealth and he is not shy about telling or showing people how wealthy he is. Freddy sometimes enjoys impressing people by actually telling them how much all his stuff is worth. Most of the time he just likes to show people he's wealthy by wearing flashy clothes and jewelry, driving expensive cars or living in an exclusive neighborhood. Freddy has a special way of thinking about money and wealth, which makes him an interesting passenger to watch on the Money Ride.

You will want to be sure to look for Suzie, Franklin, Sonya and Freddy as you rumble along grabbing and stashing dollars. As you watch them you will learn some valuable lessons which will help you make the most of every dollar you grab.

---

## Passenger Tips & Tools #4

### How Do You Value Money?

This is an important question to ask yourself as part of the process of forming sound money habits.

How do you feel money is important in your life? What specific things in your life would change or what things could you accomplish if you had more money or if you did a better job of managing your money?

Your answer will tell you two things. First it will give you an idea of what kind of Money Person you are. Second, it will help you to be more aware of your money behaviors and focus on the behaviors that make you feel good about yourself and your life.

---

## The Mechanics of Money

How exactly does money work on the Money Ride? It's not as complicated as most people think. You only have to know and remember three basic rules as you make your money decisions and choices.

### Rule 1: PAW and MAW

On the Money Ride there are only two ways to make money: (1) People at Work (PAW)—people working to earn wages or a salary called "earned income"; and (2) Money at Work (MAW)—money working to earn more money or "passive income."

The dollars you use your Work I.Q. to grab are PAW dollars. Your first challenge on the Money Ride will be to use your Work I.Q. to grab as many PAW dollars as possible—in the form of earned income.

For most people, earned income is the raw material of wealth potential. Without it, mere survival becomes a challenge and prosperity an elusive dream. So how does PAW work?

PAW is really your Work I.Q. in action. Action is the key word here because it is not enough to simply grow and nurture your Work I.Q. You must put it into action and sustain your PAW activity with consistency and discipline—it's called your work ethic.

Be aware!—there are plenty of passengers on the Money Ride who seem to have a high Work I.Q., but who don't manage to get much grabbing done. They may be educated, creative, personable etc., but they never muster the ambition, drive or discipline needed to make the action part of PAW happen. They miss out on the financial opportunities that come from optimizing their Work I.Q./PAW potential. You can't be this type of passenger *and* expect to make the most of your opportunities on the Money Ride.

As you master the dynamic of PAW, you will be able to create opportunities to use your MAW dynamic to grow wealth. MAW is really your Money I.Q. in action. Again, taking action will be the key to your success.

There will be numerous opportunities to build wealth during your turn on the Money Ride. Each opportunity will feature both promise and pitfalls…without both there would be no adventure! You will grow with every MAW decision and choice you make, as you learn to recognize and optimize your Money Ride opportunities.

### Rule 2: Money Is Limited

This rule is based upon a basic law of economics called the "Law of Scarcity." This law states that as an individual you have limited money resources with which to try and fulfill a multitude of needs and wants.

This law is universal and everyone—from the poor to the wealthy—must play by its rules. The basic difference between the poor and the wealthy is that the poor person's limited money resources are "not enough" to cover needs and wants while the wealthy person's limited supply is "more than enough."

On the Money Ride, your ultimate goal is to efficiently manage your finances so that your limited money supply is always "more than enough" money for lifetime needs and wants.

Since your money supply is limited, every decision you make with a dollar has an impact on your total money supply. When you decide to use a dollar for something, you are deciding to forego all other uses of that dollar.

According to the Law of Scarcity, this is how your money behavior affects your total money supply. The impact may be small or large, but it is always at work and it should be considered in every decision.

This impact of each dollar choice you make on the rest of your money supply is like the energy created when you push over the first in a line of dominos. The first domino knocks down the second, then third, then fourth…etc. The first domino represents the initial dollar decision. As it falls the energy created by the initial decision affects the other dominos down the line.

From small to big, the larger the decision, the greater the energy created by the first domino and the larger the number of other dollar dominos that are affected. Because your money supply is limited, it is important to pay attention to all of your dominos, not just the first one you push over.

Remember the Law of Scarcity. Your money supply consists of limited countable dollars, each with its own potential. Make the most of your first-time opportunity with each dollar and pay attention to the domino effect.

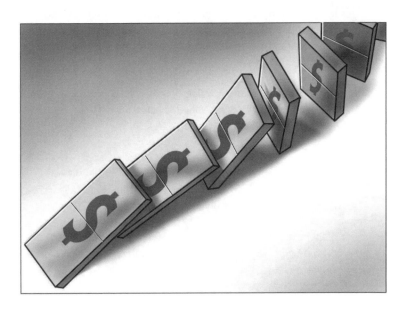

## Rule 3: Money & Time

There is a fundamental and powerful connection between money and time, which causes your Money Ride dollars to grow or decay in number and value over time. This growing and decaying is connected to another basic economic principle: The Time Value of Money.

There is a financial formula for calculating the change in money's value over time called the "Time Value of Money" formula. It is used to measure the growth and decay of money over time.

Keep in mind that math formulas are most useful for accurately measuring past changes in the value of money over time. They can also be used to project or estimate future changes in the value of money over time, but no formula can accurately predict the future value of your money.

---

 **Passenger Tips & Tools #5**

### Time Value of Money Formula:
### $FV = P(1+i)^n$

This formula can be used to measure the growth and the decay of money over time. Let's first look at how it is used to measure the decay of money. You'll learn how to use it to measure growth later in this guide.

| | |
|---|---|
| **FV** | = Future value |
| **P** | = Present value/principal |
| **i** | = Interest rate |
| **n** | = Number of time periods |

Using this formula, if you had $100 today (P) and you estimate that inflation will average –3% (i) over the next 20 years (n), what will be the future purchasing value (FV) in 20 years of your $100?

You can calculate the estimate that your $100 will be have the purchasing power of $54.38 in today dollars...inflation decay of over 45% in 20 years!

---

The connection between time and money creates two basic kinds of time-connected money and on the Money Ride we call these "Today Dollars" and "Tomorrow Dollars."

Today Dollars are dollars that are available for immediate needs or wants. Today Dollars are a product of income.

Tomorrow Dollars are dollars which need to be available for future needs and wants. Tomorrow Dollars are a product of wealth.

Each has its own particular purpose and importance in your Money Ride choices and decisions. This means that when you spend Today Dollars, it will be important to always be aware of the need to accumulate Tomorrow Dollars.

There are tips and tools throughout this guide which will help you make smart money decisions in order to maintain a proper balance in your supply of Today Dollars and Tomorrow Dollars.

## PAW and MAW

On the Money Ride the good and bad potential of the relationship between time and money is always at work, operating through two basic money dynamics: the "PAW Dynamic" and the "MAW Dynamic."

The PAW dynamic is about harvesting—grabbing Money Ride dollars. PAW's impact on your financial success will quickly become obvious to you in your grabbing efforts as you apply your Work I.Q. to gather as many dollars as you can.

It won't be enough to just work hard at the grabbing, you'll have to learn to work smart at the grabbing as well. Working smart makes the work less difficult and more productive.

As you fine tune your Work I.Q. on the Money Ride, you will have the opportunity to continually increase your income by figuring out more efficient ways to grab dollars.

The MAW dynamic is about storing and utilizing your harvest of PAW dollars. You will learn to make smart money decisions with your crop of fresh PAW dollars to create a continuous supply of MAW dollars for wealth building.

Efficiency is just as important in utilizing your MAW dollars as it is in harvesting PAW dollars. This is where your Money I.Q. will take over the stewardship of your wealth building efforts. Your financial success will ultimately be determined by how and where you apply your MAW dollars to create wealth.

Each of these dynamics has the potential to increase your lifetime money supply. Each is also vulnerable to economic forces and events whose impact can decrease your lifetime money supply.

This positive and negative potential is influenced by the Law of Scarcity, the Time Value of Money and the fact that money is a commodity.

## Money Decay

Since money is a commodity, like all commodities its value can be affected over time by a variety of decaying factors. On the Money Ride, your ability to minimize, neutralize or eliminate the exposure to the decaying factors will be a valuable wealth-building skill.

Consider for example, another commodity—corn. What happens if corn is left in the field exposed to the forces of nature? It will of course, wither and decay or be consumed by pests. However, if the corn is properly harvested, carefully stored and efficiently processed, it can be used to produce a variety of products from food to fuel.

So, what are the factors that will cause the amount and value of your PAW and MAW dollars to decay and how do they work?

There are two levels of decay which occur. The first level is the decrease in the purchasing value of each individual dollar in your money supply. This first level of decay is caused by inflation.

Inflation is essentially the dilution of the economy's money supply caused by the government increasing the number of dollars in circulation. When the number of dollars in circulation increases, the purchasing value of each dollar decreases—a dollar won't buy as much as it used to. This is due to the fact that there are more dollars available to spend relative to the number of goods available to buy.

The second level of decay is the decrease in the amount of dollars you have available—the purchasing value of your total money supply. This second level of decay is caused by three basic forces: taxes, fluctuating financial markets and spending.

Each of these second level factors can reduce your money supply in two ways. First, they reduce the total amount of Today Dollars you have. Second, because they cause a loss of Today Dollars, you also miss out on the Tomorrow Dollars that your lost Today Dollars might have become.

Taxes are essentially the transaction fees you are obligated to pay as a citizen. There are five different types of taxes that your PAW and MAW dollars could be exposed to on the Money Ride: income taxes, property taxes, sales taxes, capital gains taxes and gift & estate taxes.

You'll pay income taxes as a percentage of the income you earn. You'll pay a sales tax as a percentage of the price of certain goods and services you buy. You'll pay a property tax on the value of real estate you own. You'll pay a capital gains tax as a percentage of the gain you earn when you sell an investment for a profit. Finally, you may have to pay a gift & estate tax on assets that you transfer to your family during your lifetime and at your death.

Because taxes are part of so many transactions, it is always important to consider the potential tax impact on your money supply in every financial decision. In some cases you will not be able to avoid paying a tax. However, in many cases, you can manage your tax exposure by planning the timing, amount or way in which you earn, spend and invest. In these cases, when it comes to taxes, ignorance of the rules can cost you money by unknowingly paying more in taxes than the law requires you to pay.

**Passenger Tips & Tools #6**

### Are You Smart About Your Taxes?

It's important to know when you might be obligated to pay taxes, but you don't have to become an expert to be "tax smart."

In the early stage of your turn on the Money Ride, your financial situation will likely be simple enough that you can prepare your own income tax return. There are many free or inexpensive internet resources for this level of "do it yourself" tax planning.

But as your earnings increase and you begin to acquire assets, your tax situation will become more complicated. This is when being "smart" often means getting help from a tax expert. The fee you pay for an expert's advice will be worth the money you save by avoiding unnecessary taxes.

Fluctuating financial markets can cause the value of your assets to decrease in value. Periodic changes in market value are normal and they usually are associated with changes in the overall economy. The key is to understand that you have no control over market fluctuations. You must therefore consider their potential impact when deciding where and how to put your MAW dollars to work.

The decay caused by spending involves two basic types of expenses: lifestyle and financial emergencies. Lifestyle spending covers housing food, clothes, transportation and everything else you need to live. Emergencies are what they sound like—unexpected events that cost an unpredictable amount.

All lifestyle spending reduces your money supply, but the most destructive form of lifestyle spending is Stupid Spending ($-S^2$). Stupid Spending includes buying something you can't afford, paying too much or buying solely on impulse. The kind of Money Person you are and your money behavior will determine the amount of dollar decay that occurs due to lifestyle maintenance, especially when it comes to $-S^2$.

Financial emergencies will happen and you must allow for them in your planning. If you don't, the money an emergency costs could seriously derail your pursuit of financial success on the Money Ride.

It's almost time! The roar of the roller coaster is deafening now, and as you catch a glimpse inside, you see that there is money swirling everywhere.

Time for one last quick check of what's been covered so far in your passenger's guide. You're clear on the Grabbing Rules—check. You've explored the Uses of Money and have an idea of what kind of Money Person you are—check. And you know your Money Rules backwards and forwards—check!

So, what's next? Well, you're probably beginning to realize that once your turn begins, you're going to be grabbing all these dollars and you're going to need a system for stashing and growing them. Read on, because the next section of your guide addresses this important challenge.

# 4. Stashing Your Cash

## The Opportunity Vest

Regardless of whether you will be using just your hands or the biggest of nets to do your grabbing, you will need somewhere to store all the Money Ride dollars that you will be gathering. You are going to need something a whole lot bigger than your pockets, wallet or purse to do the job.

No problem—every passenger on the Money Ride gets their very own custom-fitted Opportunity Vest which features specially-designed pockets for storing and deploying your Grabbing Dollars.

Your Opportunity Vest is where your Money I.Q. takes over for your Work I.Q., much like a runner in a relay race passes the baton to a teammate. With every grabbed dollar you stash in your vest you are passing the baton from your Work I.Q. to your Money I.Q.

The vest has three pockets on the front and two large pockets which cover the entire back of the vest. The three front pockets are labeled "SPEND," "SAVE" and "INVEST." The back pockets are labeled "PROTECT" and "BORROW." The vest pockets are elastic and will expand and shrink with your money supply based upon the money decisions you make with each dollar.

In addition to being expandable, each of your vest pockets serves a particular use of money. However, regardless of their specific use, all of the pockets operate according to the fundamental uses and mechanics of money explained earlier in this guide.

Because the pockets all operate according to the same money fundamentals, there is a dynamic connection between them. Remember the domino effect? This is the dynamic link between your money decisions and the dollars in the vest pockets. Based upon the law of scarcity, what you do with a dollar in one pocket has the potential to affect the amount or the value of the dollars in your other pockets.

## Vest Dynamics

Your Opportunity Vest is designed to help you with two important jobs: organizing your money and using your money effectively.

The vest pockets make it possible to organize your money supply according to the intended use for each dollar. This organization will help you avoid two common and related financial pitfalls which can jeopardize your financial success.

The first pitfall is mentally spending money you have not yet received. The second pitfall is mistakenly planning more than one use for the same dollar.

Allocating portions of your money supply in a particular pocket according to a specific use will enable you to better utilize each dollar. This efficient use of your money is especially important because your money supply is limited as described by the scarcity of money principle.

The number of dollars in each of the pockets will always be the combined product of your money decisions and the factors which decay the value of money. The combination of this deciding and decaying will create money activity throughout your vest pockets.

The money activity throughout your Opportunity Vest happens in two stages. The first stage is using your Work I.Q. to grab and stash as many PAW dollars as possible. The second stage is using your Money I.Q. to efficiently deploy dollars in the various pockets to maintain cash flow and create wealth.

You will continually be challenged to use your money efficiently. This will involve using your Opportunity Vest to deploy your dollars throughout the vest pockets to grow your money supply. You will learn through experience as you are presented with a sometimes dizzying assortment of financial decisions and choices. As long as you are focused and efficient with your grabbing as well as your stashing, you will always have pockets full of money to deal with whatever opportunities and challenges come your way on the Money Ride.

The remaining sections of this guide will cover in detail the purpose and dynamics of each vest pocket. In addition to the pocket details, you will find examples of how fellow passengers deal with the same financial issues and concerns that you will be facing. You'll then be able to reflect on these examples as you watch how people around you on the ride are behaving with their money.

The line is moving faster now—on to the SPEND pocket!

# 5. The Spend Pocket

## PAW at Work

You'll remember from the previous section on money dynamics that PAW is one of the two fundamental ways to make money.

PAW dollars come from using your Work I.Q. to grab and stash dollars.

The SPEND pocket is the required and automatic first stop for every PAW dollar that you grab on the Money Ride. The decisions you make in this pocket are crucial to your financial success…today and tomorrow.

The money activity in the SPEND pocket is where your wealth-building potential begins. In this pocket you will make a pivotal decision with every dollar you grab.

It's really quite logical and simple. Since your money supply is finite, the first decision you make with every Grabbing Dollar that passes through your hands is "to spend or not to spend."

It's called "spending less than you earn" and it is a simple yet powerful dynamic that empowers you to make an important transition with your money from PAW to MAW.

The transition involves effectively combining your Work I.Q. for grabbing PAW dollars with your Money I.Q. for deploying MAW dollars to build wealth. In order to achieve financial success you have to know how to get from PAW to MAW. On the Money Ride, this is called bridging the gap between PAW and MAW.

Imagine two cliffs labeled "PAW" and "MAW" separated by a bottomless chasm. This is the "Chasm of Financial Despair" and it's filled with financial mistakes, bad habits and missed opportunities. Your challenge is to build and maintain a bridge across the chasm—a "Wealth Bridge" to get you from PAW to MAW. It's an exciting and harrowing task, but you won't have to go it alone because you'll have help.

## Your Friend Bud

Meet Bud, the friendly Money Ride attendant. When it comes to building your Wealth Bridge from PAW to MAW—do not fear because Bud is here! Bud will help you get from PAW to MAW—Bud-get! That's right, your Wealth Bridge from PAW to MAW is called a "budget."

Your budget is your personal, customized spending plan which will provide you with an organized and systematic approach to making smart "to spend or not to spend" decisions.

It's Bud's job to show you how to build and maintain your Wealth Bridge across the Chasm of Financial Despair. Don't worry about the chasm, just stay mindful of the opportunity or Wealth Bridge benefit of building and maintaining a budget. Every smart spending decision you make represents another sturdy plank in your Wealth Bridge.

Before we get into the "how" of building and maintaining your budget, you need to understand and appreciate the money dynamics behind the "why" of your budget.

The key to your success in the SPEND pocket will be to consciously make spending decisions with a purpose or plan rather than unconsciously by habit without a purpose or plan.

There are many passengers who don't recognize the difference between conscious and unconscious spending. They live only for earning and spending PAW dollars and they get nowhere on the Money Ride.

The big problem with passengers who practice unconscious spending, is that it costs them in two ways. First, it costs PAW dollars as they live from paycheck to paycheck spending all that they earn. Second, it costs MAW dollars because they end up with no extra PAW dollars which can be converted to MAW dollars to build wealth.

Bud's purpose on the Money Ride is to help you use a budget to develop and maintain the sound money habit of smart spending. This will enable you to effectively manage your PAW dollars to create MAW dollars. The MAW dollars will then drive financial opportunities in the other Opportunity Vest pockets.

You see, Smart Spending $(+S^2)$—spending less than you earn—is how MAW dollars are first created. These MAW dollars can then be put to work throughout the other pockets of your Opportunity Vest to create wealth.

As you will discover in the next chapter, the real challenge with budgeting is not about the numbers—it's about your personal commitment.

## Budget = D²

There are a number of different ways to design a budget. The most important thing to remember when it comes to a budget is that your behavior is more critical than the design. There is a very simple Money Ride formula to help you remember this important point:

$$\text{BUDGET} = \text{DISCRETION} \times \text{DISCIPLINE}$$

Discretion is the thought you put into making your "to spend or not to spend" choices and decisions. Discipline is sticking to the spending plan that is based on your budget. Discretion and discipline are the foundation of your budget because these two D's enable you to control your money.

Controlling your money is important because *if you don't control it, it will control you.* That's why a budget is such an important tool.

In order for Bud to help you gain control over your spending, you must first know what kind of Money Person you are. Are you a Suzie, Franklin, Sonya or Freddy? If you are unsure about the type of passenger you are, think about the roles money plays in your life.

What is the most important use of money to you? Are you careful about how much you pay for things? Do you worry about what your friends think about how you dress or where you live or the car you drive? Does having a bunch of money set aside make you feel good?

How you answer these questions will tell you what kind of Money Person you are. Once you know, you can begin to build a sensible budget that you can live with. The Money Person you are greatly influences how you exercise discretion in managing your PAW dollars.

## Spending a Dollar

TAXES 20%

FOOD 11%

HOUSING 26%

CLOTHING 3%

TRANSPORTATION 13%

HEALTH CARE 5%

ENTERTAINNMENT 4%

EDUCATION 2%

CHARITY 3%

RETIREMENT 8%

MISC. 5%

**Passenger Tips & Tools #7**

### Are You S.M.A.R.T. About Your Goals?

1. Write a description of what it is you want as though you already have it. Be **Specific** about what it is and how it feels to know you have accomplished it.
2. List the steps you will need to take to achieve your goal. The steps must be **Measurable** so that you can track your progress...how much...how many, etc.
3. Develop a "can do" attitude about achieving your goal... know that you are deserving of what it is you want and be confident that your goal is **Attainable**.
4. Be **Realistic** about your goal. Be clear that it is something that you are both determined and able to accomplish. Aim high and be real.
5. Give yourself a deadline for achieving your goal so that it is **Timely** in terms of your current situation.

Once you have figured out what kind of Money Person you are, the next influence on your budget will be your lifestyle and life goals. Your lifestyle will require spending Today Dollars, while your life goals will require a supply of Tomorrow Dollars. This means that if you spend all of your Today Dollars on your lifestyle you won't have enough Tomorrow Dollars to fulfill your life goals.

The amount of discretion you have in managing your spending will depend upon how well you balance your lifestyle needs and life goals. Let's first explore the impact of your life goals on your budget.

Divide your life goals into two basic categories—short term and long term. Short-term goals are for those things you want to accomplish in twelve months or less. Long-term goals are the things you want to accomplish beyond one year. Regardless of the time frame for completion, life goals cost something. The cost involves either spending Today Dollars for short-term goals or Tomorrow Dollars for long-term goals.

Budget planning for life goals is a continuous process. Some goals are completed, while others change before they are completed.

Regardless of the pace of goal completion or the frequency of goal change, your life goals will present a continuous budget challenge where discretion is important. The challenge is to efficiently managing your money to pay the cost of short-term goals while simultaneously generating enough money to pay the cost of your long-term goals.

This challenge will at times mean spending Today Dollars and maybe also Tomorrow Dollars. At other times it will mean going without some comforts or luxuries in order to generate more Tomorrow Dollars for future goals.

Now let's talk about the second major influence on the design and content of your budget—your lifestyle.

The lifestyle you choose will obviously cost money to live. What kind of lifestyle do you want to live, and what kind of lifestyle can you afford to live?

This is where discretion again becomes your most important tool in maintaining balance between your ideal world—where and how you ultimately want to live—and your real world—where and how you can afford to live today. The challenge is to have both without sacrificing one for the other.

Now, let's talk about the second D in BUDGET = $D^2$—discipline. As important as discretion is in all of your Money Ride choices and decisions, its effectiveness comes from its partnership with discipline.

This partnership brings consistency to your spending plan by keeping your discretion focused on the balance between your lifestyle and your life goals. Discipline is the glue that holds your budget together, enabling you to enjoy a continuous flow of Today Dollars and Tomorrow Dollars.

## Building Your Budget

The first step in designing your budget is understanding that the purpose of the SPEND pocket is to efficiently manage the supply of PAW dollars you grab. This means that you have to allocate your inflow of PAW dollars to cover the outflow for expenses, savings and investments.

The initial outflow from the SPEND pocket becomes the inflow to the other pockets on your vest. This begins a constant money activity of inflow and outflow throughout your vest pockets. This money activity is called "cash flow" and it is what ultimately drives wealth building.

Your budget will be a valuable tool that will enable you to effectively manage your cash flow. This process converts PAW dollars into MAW dollars which in turn will be used to build wealth.

---

 **Passenger Tips & Tools #8**

### Tracking Your Spending

Here is a convenient way to keep track of what you spend:

- Purchase two receipt spindles and put them on a kitchen counter where you will see them every day.
- Save all of your purchase receipts.
- Put the receipts from all cash purchases on one spindle and those from credit card purchases on the other.
- At the end of the month, use the receipts to complete your budget.

---

### Step 1

The actual budget design work begins with making a single column list of income and expenses. Income will usually be a single item labeled "Take Home Pay." Expenses will be broken down into two major categories: "Needs" at the top and "Wants" at the bottom.

Needs are basic lifestyle items which include groceries, housing, clothes, transportation, health and emergency cash reserves. Wants are everything else, such as entertainment, vacations and future life goals.

Keep in mind that everyone's list of needs and wants looks different. Your list will be determined by the type of Money Person you are and your lifestyle.

Next, divide the needs and wants into two-sub groups: "Fixed" and "Variable." Fixed expenses in each major category are those expenses which require spending the same amount of money each month. Variable expenses are those expenses where the amount of money spent each month changes, based on price fluctuation or how much of an item is used or consumed.

Once your list of needs and wants—with the breakdown of fixed and variable—is complete, you're ready for the final structural elements of your budget: the "Target" and "Month" columns.

## Step 2

In the Target column first you will enter the monthly amount for each fixed Needs and Wants item. Next you will enter an estimate for the monthly amount that you expect to spend on each variable Needs and Wants expense item.

## Step 3

Next, to the right of the Target column, you can create the Month column for recording the actual monthly expense amount for each Needs and Wants item.

If you want to keep track of more than one month's spending, create multiple Month columns to the right of the Target column. You could also include an "Annual" column as the last column to the far right to keep track of your spending for an entire year.

Your budget form is now designed and ready to help you organize and deploy your Grabbing Dollars.

At the end of each month you will enter the actual amount spent on each expense item for that month. At the end of a twelve-month period, the sum of the monthly totals for each expense item is entered in the Total Year column.

The dollar amounts you enter in the "Target" column will provide you with a benchmark value for each expense item. Each month you can then compare your actual expenses to their respective benchmarks.

This comparison of Target to the actual monthly amounts spent is a handy tool for monitoring your cash flow. It is also useful for

# Sample Monthly Budget

| | Target Amount | Actual January | Actual February | Actual March | Total Year |
|---|---|---|---|---|---|
| Take-Home Pay | 1,800 | 1,800 | 1,800 | 1,800 | 21,600 |
| **NEEDS** | | | | | |
| *Fixed Expenses* | | | | | |
| Savings—MAW | 100 | 100 | 100 | 100 | 1,200 |
| Rent | 300 | 300 | 300 | 300 | 3,600 |
| Car Payments | 250 | 250 | 250 | 250 | 3,000 |
| Phone | 35 | 35 | 35 | 38 | 420 |
| Health Insurance | 75 | 75 | 75 | 75 | 420 |
| Other/Misc | | | | | |
| *Variable Expenses* | | | | | |
| Food | 300 | 250 | 200 | 225 | 2,650 |
| Auto Gas/Repairs | 150 | 100 | 75 | 175 | 1,200 |
| Utilities | 85 | 82 | 80 | 94 | 996 |
| Clothing | 25 | 50 | 0 | 80 | 550 |
| Credit Card Payments | 0 | 25 | 0 | 30 | 175 |
| Other/Misc | | | | | |
| **Needs Subtotal** | **1,320** | **1,267** | **1,115** | **1,364** | **14,691** |
| **WANTS** | | | | | |
| *Fixed Expenses* | | | | | |
| Memberships | 50 | 50 | 50 | 50 | 600 |
| Subscriptions | 15 | 15 | 15 | 15 | 180 |
| Lessons | | | | | |
| Vacation Fund | 100 | 100 | 100 | 100 | 1,200 |
| Other/Misc | | | | | |
| *Variable Expenses* | | | | | |
| Food/Dining Out | 100 | 50 | 65 | 120 | 450 |
| Entertainment/Recreation | 100 | 125 | 72 | 53 | 364 |
| Credit Card Payments | 0 | 25 | 30 | 0 | 210 |
| Other/Misc | | | | | |
| **Wants Subtotal** | **365** | **365** | **332** | **338** | **3,004** |
| **Needs Subtotal (as above)** | **1,320** | **1,267** | **1,115** | **1,364** | **14,691** |
| **Total Wants & Needs** | **1,685** | **1,632** | **1,447** | **1,702** | **17,695** |
| **Net Income to savings** | **115** | **168** | **353** | **98** | **3,905** |

**Passenger Tips & Tools #9**

### Your Budget—
### Do You Really Have to Write it Down?

Yes and No…there are many free or inexpensive budget applications on the internet which you can use to design and maintain a budget on your computer or PDA.

However, it is still smart to write it down first…pencil and paper. It will ultimately save you time and you will find it easier to mentally maintain a "sense of budget" as you go through your daily money decisions.

observing how the kind of Money Person you are influences your spending patterns.

You will use your budget data to evaluate how efficiently you deploy your PAW money to balance your spending between your lifestyle and your life goals. You'll be able to tell which spending developments were within your control and which were not.

You then will be able to use this information to make adjustments to your budget to improve the PAW-to-MAW efficiency in your SPEND pocket. This flexibility to make adjustments as things change in your life is important to maintaining your lifestyle and pursuing your life goals.

Your budget will serve as your structured, yet flexible spending plan, based upon discretion and discipline. It will help you to use the power of "spend less than you earn" to generate a continuous cash flow of MAW dollars for building wealth.

Now it's time to reap the rewards of the sound money habit of smart spending (+S²)—on to the SAVE pocket!

**Passenger Watch**

### D² Anyone?

All the Suzie's and Freddy's on the Money Ride love their SPEND pocket!

Suzie lives to spend and at the rate she burns through money, she will never see the MAW side of the chasm…but sadly she doesn't yet realize that her overspending will lead to nowhere for lack of a wealth bridge.

Freddy, yes, he definitely knows how to spend money, but unlike Suzie he is aware of his limits…most of the time. He has to be careful to avoid the temptation of always needing the latest and greatest gizmo or gadget.

There are also some Freddys on the ride that really can't afford to be a Freddy, but they love showing off. They will find out later the true cost of pretending.

Sonya and Franklin always keep their D² well focused in the SPEND pocket.

Sonya always has another investment in mind and wants to spend as little as possible to leave more for investing.

Franklin is the king of budgeting. He keep careful track of every penny. But he gets carried away with penny pinching at times and forgets to take time to treat himself to some fun.

# 6. The Save Pocket

## Here Comes MAW

The SAVE pocket is the first stop for the MAW dollars created by smart spending ($+S^2$) in your SPEND pocket. These MAW dollars are your reward for sticking to your budget.

Now that you are safely across the chasm, your MAW dollars serve their first two important purposes in your SAVE pocket.

The first purpose is to provide a lifestyle safety net for unexpected expenses and emergencies. These MAW dollars are called "reserves."

The second purpose is funding short-term life goals. These are goals with a duration of four years or less. The MAW dollars used to fund them are called "goald."

Once you have fully funded these two purposes, any of your additional MAW dollars can be put to work in the INVEST pocket.

## Save = Safe

This is the basic SAVE pocket formula, and like the budget formula from the SPEND pocket, it is obviously not math. Since the money in your SAVE pocket is intended to establish your safe foothold, it is called "safe money."

Safe money is essentially what its name suggests, but it has three aspects to its definition—location, risk and liquidity.

Location has two dimensions: (1) institution—the financial institution where you deposit your MAW money; and (2) account— a record of how much you have deposited with the institution.

On the Money Ride, institution means "bank." There many kinds of institutions such as banks, credit unions and savings & loans, but in the SAVE pocket they are all considered banks.

Think of an "account" as your personal bag of money at the bank. There are different types of bags with different features. You will be able to choose, according to your saving objective, which type of bag(s) you use to store the money in your account.

Risk is the chance that you may lose money. A loss can result from downward fluctuations in the economy, financial markets or the value of a specific account. In the SAVE pocket, risk is to be avoided at all times. You will learn later in this section about how your SAVE pocket money can be protected from risk.

Liquidity is the ease with which your MAW money accounts can be converted to cash on demand. Liquidity is an important consideration with every SAVE pocket account you establish. You want to be able to get cash when you need it.

The "Save = Safe" formula is a reminder, telling you to look for safety and liquidity when you stash your MAW dollars in your SAVE pocket. Just remember that with every MAW dollar in your SAVE pocket, safety is the first requirement.

As with every pocket on your Opportunity Vest, the dollars you stash in your SAVE pocket will require you to choose and decide. There are three basic questions you will have to answer with the MAW dollars you'll be vesting in your SAVE pocket:

1. How much?
2. How soon/How long?
3. Where?

These questions are interdependent, and the answers will change with your circumstances as you travel along on the Money Ride.

## How Much?

"How much?" is the first and most important question you must answer with your MAW dollars in the SAVE pocket. Because it is the most important question, it is sometimes also the most challenging. This is because "How much?" must also take into account "How soon/How long?" your SAVE pocket dollars may be needed.

In order to form good SAVE pocket money habits, it is important to treat saving each month as though it were an expense. This means designating an amount for savings in the Target column of your budget each month for MAW dollars.

The amount you choose as your SAVE pocket target will depend upon the amount of PAW money you grab, the cost of your lifestyle and the anticipated cost of fulfilling your goals.

A good first target for reserves would be an amount equal to your total lifestyle expenses for one month. The next reserves target would be three months' expenses. Your final reserves target would be six to twelve months' expenses.

As an example, let's say that you allocate at least 10% each month of your PAW dollars to your "MAW dollar expense." After ten months of budgeting you would then have the equivalent of one month's total income stashed in your SAVE pocket.

Once you have figured out the reserves amount, you'll then decide how much goald money you need for goals. While you will have short-term and long-term goals, only goald for short-term goals is stashed in the SAVE pocket. You will learn about stashing goald for long-term goals later in the INVEST pocket.

 **Passenger Tips & Tools #10**

### What's Your Savings Target?

Think of savings as paying yourself first...setting money aside for you before you spend your first dollar each month.

What percentage of your take-home income should you save each month? 10% is a good beginning target amount for establishing a sound money habit of saving.

But if you want to stay ahead of taxes, inflation and the other economic factors that can cause your money supply to decay, 20% should be your savings goal.

The price and the completion schedule for each goal will dictate the amount you will need to have vested in your SAVE pocket for the things you want to accomplish in your life.

Each short-term goal has its own cost and importance determined by your life priorities. First you will have to determine the amount of goald needed for each goal. Then the challenge will be to maintain a consistent flow of MAW dollars into the SAVE pocket to fund each goal.

Your target amount for all short-term goals should be part of your MAW dollars expense in your monthly budget. This will ensure that sufficient PAW dollars are converted to MAW dollars every month to cover the cost of your short-term goals.

Now that you know how to answer the "How much?" question, you're ready to move on to the next SAVE pocket question: "How soon/How long?"

---

 **Passenger Tips & Tools #11**

### How Liquid is Your Savings Account?

**Basic Savings & Money Market**—You can withdraw cash from your account on demand anytime with no penalty or fee for withdrawal.

**Certificate of Deposit**—Has a specified minimum holding time (e.g. 30 days – 2 years) before you can withdraw cash without paying an early withdrawal penalty. If you withdraw cash early, you forfeit interest you would have earned if you had waited until the maturity date.

---

## How Soon/How Long?

After "How Much?" comes the "How soon/How long?" question. The first part of the question deals with the liquid aspect of your SAVE pocket money: How soon do you need it, and how quickly can it be converted to cash?

How soon might you need to rely on your SAVE pocket reserves to help you through a financial emergency or take advantage of a financial opportunity? The timing is as impossible to predict as the amount, which makes having liquid dollars so essential.

This is why it is so important to start stashing dollars in your SAVE pocket as soon and as regularly as possible.

Now that you realize that you might need to depend on your savings at any moment, the next question is how long might you need to rely on your savings to serve as or supplement your sole source of income?

What if you wanted to take advantage of a life opportunity which required that you move to a different city, state or country? How much would it cost to relocate, start your new life and live until your first paycheck arrives?

What about emergencies? What if because of an illness or injury you couldn't work for a while? How many months of living expenses might you need until you recover?

Finally, what about your life goals, like education, buying a home, buying a car, starting a new job or changing careers? All of these represent a potential need for MAW dollars/goald to satisfy a short-term goal.

Regardless of whether it involves reserves or goald, there will be times on the Money Ride when you will have to deal with the "How soon/How long?" question.

Now on to the last SAVE pocket question—"Where?"

## Where?

The best place to put the MAW dollars you stash in your SAVE pocket is in a bank. On the Money Ride, a "bank" is any financial institution authorized and regulated by the government to store people's savings. So, the term "bank" includes savings and loans, credit unions, banks and online banks, to name a few.

Banks may differ in name or type, but they all perform the same two basic functions—storing money and lending money. They provide storing and lending services by taking in deposits from customers and using the deposits to make loans to other customers. So, when you store your MAW dollars, you are making a short-term loan to the institution.

Banks attract deposit money by paying you a fee to store your MAW dollars there. This fee is called "interest" and it is measured in percentages called "interest rates." The institution then takes deposit money and lends it to other customers and charges them an interest fee to borrow it.

---

 **Passenger Tips & Tools #12**

### How Safe Is Your Money?

All banks offer deposit accounts where the safety of your money is guaranteed by the government through the Federal Deposit Insurance Corporation (FDIC). The FDIC guarantees the safety of a passenger's account up to $250,000 per bank.

---

You earn a profit on your money based on the interest you get for loaning your SAVE pocket money to the institution. In turn, the institution earns its profit by charging other people a higher interest rate to borrow your money than they pay you to store it.

The longer you agree to leave your money in an account with a financial institution, the higher interest rate you should expect to be paid for the use of your money. This is the basic contract or deal you make with a financial institution when you give it your MAW dollars for safekeeping.

Since the interest your money earns is your incentive to store money with a financial institution, it is important to understand how it works.

The money you earn for storing your SAVE money is calculated using a special type of math formula called "compounding." With compounding, the financial institution pays you interest for the period of time they store your money. The interest you earn each period is added to your account value.

The rate of interest you earn is based on a yearly rate. The yearly rate is then divided into daily interest increments. For each day your money is stored, you earn a daily fraction of the yearly interest.

The advantage of compounding is that you not only earn in-

**Passenger Tips & Tools #13**

### Compounding Formula:
### $FV = P(1+i)^n$

The compounding formula is also known as the "Time Value of Money Formula." It is the only Money Ride formula that is based on actual math.

**FV** = Future value
**P** = Present value/principal
**i** = Interest rate
**n** = Number of time periods

Using this formula, if you deposited $100 PAW dollars in a savings account at 5% interest for ten years, your MAW dollars in the account would grow to $162.89.

terest on your money, you also earn interest on your interest. Each period, you also earn interest on the interest you earned in the prior period—this is compounding in action. Compounding is the domino effect of saving, and this is why your SAVE pocket money qualifies as "Money at Work."

 **Passenger Tips & Tools #14**

### The Rule of 72

If you want to know how long it will take for compounding to double the value of your PAW dollars, divide "72" by the interest rate your money will earn.

**Example:** If the bank offers to pay you 7.2% interest annually on your money, it will take how many years for your money to double in value?

### $72 \div 7.2 = 10$

It will take ten years for your money to double if you earn 7.2% interest each year.

In addition to compounding, there is a second type of interest formula that you should be aware of, called "simple interest." This type of interest is rarely used, but it deserves mention so that you are able to make smart SAVE pocket money decisions if you are offered this option.

Simple interest is, as its name suggests, simple. Unlike compounding, simple interest is paid each period on the principal only. There is no interest earned on the interest.

While compound and simple interest produce different results, they share a common dynamic—the higher the interest rate, the faster your MAW dollars grow each year.

Interest rates are important, but they are not the only factor to consider in selecting a financial institution. Another important consideration is the type of account in which you choose to store your SAVE pocket money.

---

 **Passenger Tips & Tools #9**

**Simple Interest Formula:**
**FV = P + (P x i x n)**

From the prior example you know that $100 will grow to $162.89 in ten years at 5% using compounding.

If you use the simple interest formula to calculate the interest earned, you would end up with $150.00 after ten years.

The longer the period or higher the interest, the greater the difference in ending value would be.

---

There will be many different types of savings programs to choose from, such as money market accounts, savings accounts, treasury bills and certificates of deposit. The "How soon/How long?" question will influence your choice because these accounts store money for different lengths of time. Your choice will mean matching your short-term and long-term savings goals with an appropriately timed savings account.

The process of matching your savings goals to the specific type of account is called "staging." Staging involves positioning your MAW dollars in an order that reflects when you will need a particular amount of your SAVE dollars for a particular purpose.

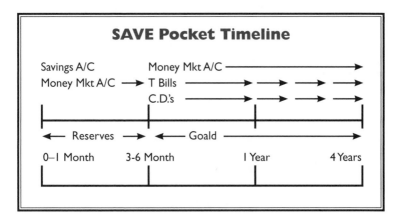

Think of this staging visually as a timeline of MAW money in your SAVE pocket that matches your timeline of cash needs. Accounts designated for reserves would be at the left end of the timeline. Those designated for goald would be located along the timeline from left (short term) to right (long term).

Accounts for storing reserves would be those positioned on the left in savings accounts or money market accounts. Goald account money for life goals a year or more in the future would be positioned from left to right on the timeline in treasury bills and certificates of deposit. This approach ensures that an adequate amount of SAVE money is always available when it is needed for emergencies, opportunities and short-term goals.

It is important to realize that not much wealth building will take place in your SAVE pocket because of the relationship between time and money. The MAW dollars stored in your SAVE pocket will be there for a limited amount of time. Since interest earned is a function of the rate and the number of periods it is earned, SAVE pocket dollars don't generate a lot of interest earnings. This is because the interest rate is typically too low and earnings period too short to take full advantage of compound interest.

Real wealth-building, based on time and money, happens in your INVEST pocket, where you will learn to work with larger amounts of MAW dollars over longer periods of time.

So, the sooner you stash the appropriate amount of MAW dollars in your SAVE pocket, the sooner you can move on to the challenges, excitement and rewards waiting for you in the INVEST pocket.

No time to waste—on to the INVEST pocket!

 **Passenger Watch**

### Is It Worth Saving?

Suzie naturally struggles with saving because she spends all and sometimes more than she earns every month. Her only incentive for saving is her next big purchase.

Sonya loves investing and because she understands risk, she knows how important reserves are. Sonya accumulated her six month reserves in less than a year so that she could start investing as soon as possible.

Franklin's saving habits are much like Sonya's but his motives are more about safety and stability than maximizing his investment opportunities. He carefully tracks his savings percentage each month and is very careful about where and how he stashes his savings.

Freddy is actually very good at saving because he knows his savings are his safety net for maintaining his lifestyle and image.

# 7. The Invest Pocket

## MAW Goes to Work

The INVEST pocket is where your ability to create MAW dollars through the efficient use of money in your SPEND and SAVE pockets is rewarded. This is where your MAW dollars apply their real wealth-building muscle.

Once you begin stashing MAW dollars in your INVEST pocket, the focus of your Money I.Q. shifts from smart spending and saving to making the most of investment opportunities to build wealth.

---

 **Passenger Tips & Tools #16**

### Successful Investing Takes a Lot of D²

Before you invest, remember how hard you had to work to grab your PAW dollars and how much D² it took to create your first MAW dollars.

You will need an equal amount of discretion and discipline to design an effective investment strategy and stay with it for the long run. So, respect your MAW dollars for the hard work and D² they represent by always being vigilant and diligent in managing your investments.

---

The opportunities will be many and varied, and your financial success will depend on your ability to make informed choices. This means you have to know how an investment works, how well it suits your objectives and whether it's compatible with the type of Money Person you are.

Before we get into the specifics of how the INVEST pocket works, it's important that you have an understanding about the INVEST pocket's fundamental purpose: wealth—what it is and what it means to you.

## Wealth

On the Money Ride there are two kind of wealth: Financial Wealth and Personal Wealth.

Financial wealth is the market value of assets and the income generated by assets. The income provides cash flow to live on. The market value provides financial stability and the potential for future growth. Financial wealth is measured in dollars—Today Dollars and Tomorrow Dollars.

When you retire and you're no longer grabbing PAW dollars, your wealth assets must generate MAW-dollar income to replace the PAW cash flow. Your MAW-dollar income is generated directly by an asset, such as rental income, interest income, stock dividends, business income etc. This MAW-dollar income is called "passive income" because you don't have to actively grab these dollars as you do with PAW dollars. Passive income is the Today Dollar value of your INVEST pocket dollars.

---

 **Passenger Tips & Tools #17**

### The Tomorrow Dollar Value of Your Money

Every Today Dollar, represented by PAW and MAW dollars in your money supply has the potential to grow if you hang on to it and efficiently put it to work. This is the Tomorrow Dollar value of your money—it's potential to build wealth in the form of assets which generate income and grow in value.

Remember…attitudes and values about wealth are personal, but the money rules and mechanics for building wealth are the same for everyone.

The primary challenge of building wealth is balancing your consumption of Today Dollars with the need to create a supply of Tomorrow Dollars.

---

In addition to the MAW-dollar income, the potential future increase in the market value of your wealth assets in turn offers the potential for increased future income. This increase in future value and income helps insulate your wealth and cash flow against the eroding effects of inflation, taxes and expenses. The potential to generate future income is the Tomorrow Dollar value of the wealth you create with your INVEST pocket dollars.

On the Money Ride, the whole point of pursuing financial success and wealth is to live a happier, more fulfilled life. This makes your definition of personal wealth as important as your definition of financial wealth.

Wealth means different things to different people based upon their personal values. Every Money Ride passenger values things in their life which money cannot buy.

Personal wealth includes aspects of your life where it is not money itself that is important, but rather the people, experiences and opportunities that having money enables you to enjoy. These may include values like supporting a family, fulfilling person goals and helping others in need.

Your personal definition of wealth influences your financial definition of wealth. Your personal definition influences the lifestyle you want to live, which in turn determines the amount of money you'll need to live. The amount of money you'll need to live will then influence how you invest your MAW dollars to generate the required cash flow.

You now have a working definition of wealth to help you focus on your INVEST pocket goals and monitor your wealth-building progress.

There are four basic dynamics at work in the INVEST pocket which make it very different from the SAVE pocket: risk, reward, growth and income. These are the roller coaster "ups and downs" of building wealth.

## Invest = Risk

You'll remember that the primary characteristic of the MAW dollars stashed in your SAVE pocket is that they are safe dollars (SAVE = Safe). This means that there is little or no danger in the SAVE pocket of losing your original MAW dollars.

However, in the INVEST pocket there is always risk—the possibility that you may lose some or all of the MAW dollars you stash there. This is what makes INVEST pocket dollars fundamentally different from SAVE pocket dollars.

Risk is also what will make the decisions you make with your MAW dollars in your INVEST pocket so important, interesting and challenging.

In order to successfully deal with risk, you must start by asking yourself two basic questions:

1. What is the type and degree of risk?
2. What is my risk tolerance?

Answering these two questions involves some "figuring" and some "feeling."

The figuring part is doing your homework to determine what risks are present in a potential investment and how much risk you can afford to take. This will involve identifying the source of risk, how it might occur, how it might be offset or avoided and ultimately how much money it may cause you to lose. This research is an important aspect of your Money I.Q.

The feeling part is being honest with yourself about how taking risks with your MAW dollars makes you feel. This is called your risk tolerance, and it is based upon how risk affects you emotionally.

Figuring and feeling are both part of every investment decision you will make on the Money Ride. So, let's explore the figuring first, then we'll talk about the feeling part of the process.

What makes risk so interesting and challenging is that there are different types or elements of risk in every investment opportunity.

There are three basic types or levels of risk which you should be aware of. Each represents a chance to make or lose precious MAW dollars, so pay attention to these when considering every investment opportunity.

# The Three Levels of Risk

## 1. The Economy

This is the "big picture" level of risk. Both the general state of the economy and the major economic factors of interest rates, inflation and financial markets can have an impact on the performance of investments.

How might the general condition of the national, state and local economy negatively impact the investment?

How might higher or lower interest rates impact the investment?

How might higher or lower rates of inflation impact the investment?

How might the trend in the financial markets for stocks, bonds, commodities or real estate impact the investment?

Generally, the performance of investments will mirror the performance of the overall economy. Interest rates, inflation rates and the financial markets serve as indicators of the health and direction of the economy and have their own particular impact on investment performance.

## 2. The Industry

Once you understand the economy's influence on risk, the next level of research involves analyzing the industry in which the investment operates.

Is the investment in a profitable and stable industry?

Is it an emerging industry with a future, an established industry with a history or a fading industry offering outmoded products or services?

Is there a current demand and/or future demand for the industry's goods and services?

Is the industry reliant on consumer spending or government spending?

These are the types of questions you need to explore when assessing the potential of investing in a particular industry.

### 3. Investment

Once you have completed your research on the risk implications of the economy and the industry involved, your last step is to analyze the risk attributed to a specific investment. This may involve investigating a company, a real estate property or an investment company that manages MAW dollars for investors.

Is it profitable, financially strong and well managed?

Is there demand for its products or services?

Is it known in its industry for some special feature or innovation?

The best candidates may not be obvious at first, but by asking the right questions, the investments with solid wealth-building potential will be easier to identify.

You'll have to do your INVEST pocket homework to learn as much as you can about every source of risk before you invest. Remember, on the Money Ride homework is fun and profitable. Smart, disciplined passengers get paid to do their INVEST pocket homework—with wealth!

You may not always be able to find the answers by yourself. The good news is that there are plenty of investment experts on the Money Ride who can help you assess the risk of any prospective investment.

After you have done the figuring work of identifying the type and degree of risk, it's time to explore the feeling aspect of risk.

If you want to maximize the wealth potential of your INVEST pocket and enjoy life, it is important to feel comfortable with the degree of risk in your investments—remember your risk tolerance.

Your risk tolerance is influenced by the kind of Money Person you are and your understanding of how money and your investments work.

The more anxious you are about losing MAW dollars, the less tolerant of risk you will be. However, by understanding more about an investment, you can reduce your risk anxiety and be more confident and comfortable with your investment choices.

Now that you are aware of how risk influences your investment decisions, it's time for you to learn about the second unique INVEST pocket dynamic: Reward.

## Invest = Reward

Your research on risk is never complete until it gives equal consideration to the dynamic of reward. Reward is the potential to make money on an investment, either from an increase in its market value (growth) or from the cash flow (income) it generates.

Risk and reward are the two sides of the investment decision coin. Since either side may result, the probability of each happening must be compared in order to make an informed investment decision.

You must research the potential reward of an investment offer just as thoroughly as you study its risk, so that you can gauge its probability as accurately as possible. Doing your homework on *both* sides of the investment decision coin will help you feel more comfortable with your investment choices.

Your understanding of the risk/reward relationship will help you intelligently expand your risk tolerance, regardless of what type of Money Person you are. This expanded tolerance will mean that more investment opportunities will qualify as appropriate choices for you.

 **Passenger Tips & Tools #18**

### Risk vs. Reward

When you evaluate the potential risks of an investment always remember that the potential rewards of the investment must be greater by a great deal.

## Invest = Growth

The overall goal of every INVEST pocket decision is to build wealth through investing. Therefore, growth is the objective with every MAW dollar you stash in your INVEST pocket. The potential for growth is what you should look for in every investment opportunity that comes your way on the Money Ride. The key to your financial success will be using your Money I.Q. to transform growth potential into real wealth.

In order to gauge your success at transforming growth potential into wealth, you first have to know how to measure growth and the wealth it produces. On the Money Ride, the wealth you create by investing MAW dollars is measured in the value of assets. An asset is defined as anything you own which has two basic characteristics: the potential to grow in value and the potential to produce income.

Any increase in an asset's market value in excess of what you originally paid for it is money gained in growth. Growth can be converted to cash by selling an investment for a profit.

The key is to invest in assets which achieve growth that is continual and consistent. This sustained growth must also be at a pace or rate sufficient to stay ahead of the factors which erode money, such as taxes, inflation, fluctuating interest rates and market declines. Only by growth outpacing these eroding factors can real wealth be created.

Another important aspect of growth you must be aware of is the element of time. The value of some investments can increase very quickly. For instance, stock share prices can change dramatically in a matter of seconds or minutes. However, growth is typically not about getting rich quickly. While there are sophisticated and aggressive investing strategies offering the potential for quick gains, the fundamentals of growth are based on long-term participation in an investment.

## Invest = Income

In addition to growth, the second valuable characteristic of investment assets is the capacity to generate income. Income is the cash generated by an investment. Income can be in the form of a dividend as with stocks, interest as with bonds or rent as with real estate. The income objective typically takes a back seat to growth in the early stages of the wealth building process. However, as you reach the end of your PAW dollar–grabbing years, generating income from your MAW dollars will become the primary objective.

 **Passenger Tips & Tools #19**

### Automatic Investing

Time and discipline are important in successful investing. So start early and try making your investment contributions automatic to sustain a disciplined investing program…time will take care of the rest.

Research investment opportunities which allow you to electronically transfer MAW dollars from you bank account each month to your investment accounts.

In order to meet this switch in emphasis from growth to income, you will have to reallocate a portion of your PAW dollars from assets that do not generate income to those that do. This means moving some of your MAW dollars into investments that generate interest, dividends, rents etc.

Though the primary objective for your MAW dollars may shift to generating income, you will still want to have some of your MAW dollars invested for growth so that you will have sufficient assets to generate future lifestyle income.

Regardless of whether your investment objective is growth or income, how much wealth you build depends upon your ability to create a steady supply of MAW dollars flowing into your INVEST pocket. Once the MAW dollars are in the INVEST pocket, your success depends on your ability to invest those dollars wisely.

Next up, we will explore the mechanics of investing so that you will be better equipped to evaluate the growth and income potential of an investment before you invest.

## Mechanics of Investing

There are three fundamental ways to put your MAW dollars to work in your INVEST pocket: Invest, Diversify and Reinvest. Regardless of which investments you choose for growing your MAW dollars, your decisions will involve one or more of these three key mechanics.

### Invest

This is the obvious purpose of your INVEST pocket. It represents the action of regularly stashing MAW dollars in your INVEST pocket as investment capital to build wealth.

The wealth you build is intended to provide a lifetime supply of Tomorrow Dollars for your future lifestyle and life goals.

The regular, systematic stashing of MAW dollars in your INVEST pocket is a sound money habit which is vital to your financial success on the Money Ride.

### Diversify

Diversification is a valuable tool for dealing with investment risk and increasing wealth-building opportunity. If you simply accumulate all of your MAW dollars in a single investment, you will always be exposed to the same type and degree of risk. You will also be limiting yourself to only one asset category or opportunity to build wealth. The single investment approach can work if you are lucky, but luck is not a reliable approach to dealing with risk or building an investment portfolio. Even if you decide to invest exclusively in a particular category of investment like real estate or stocks, it will still make sense to diversify your holdings in two or more investments within the same category.

Diversifying to mange risk involves investing in two or more investments with different risk characteristics. This approach will effectively spread your exposure to risk over the different investments, rather than concentrating all of your risk exposure in a single investment. Keep in mind that diversification does not eliminate risk, it only defuses it by exposing limited portions of your total investment dollars to any one type of risk.

Diversifying to expand wealth building opportunities involves owning a variety of either different categories of assets or different assets within a single category. The value of assets is affected differently over time by various economic factors. Each individual asset or category has its own up and down business cycle of performance. Owning a variety of assets creates a greater probability that some wealth building will always be happening somewhere in your INVEST pocket.

### Reinvest

Once you have managed to accumulate some MAW dollars in your INVEST pocket and your investments have had some time to grow in value, you will have opportunities to repeat the process. Like a farmer harvesting corn, you will be harvesting your crop of new MAW dollars which grow from the seeds of your original MAW investment capital and using it as seed to grow additional wealth.

This involves taking the profits generated by your original MAW investment capital to acquire additional investment assets.

The first step to reinvesting is to identify which investments are the most profitable. A profitable investment is simply one that becomes worth more than you paid for it. Profit is new MAW dollars created from either an increase in market value of an asset or from the income it generates. Profitable investments create new wealth building opportunities by producing new MAW dollars for reinvestment.

When an asset becomes worth more that what you paid for it, you have the opportunity to sell the asset to convert profit to cash for reinvesting. You will first have to pay a tax of on the profit you earn from selling the asset and will then have the net after tax amount available to invest.

With some types of assets like stocks, bonds or mutual funds you can convert your profit to cash by selling just a portion of your total holdings. This allows you to leave your original investment intact and reinvest the profits which are new MAW dollars.

---

 **Passenger Tips & Tools #20**

### Reinvesting Your MAW Profits

If you invest $1,000 to buy 100 shares of stock for $10/share and 10 years later it's market value increases to $20/share, the increase represents a profit of $1,000.

You could then sell 50 shares for $20/share, generating $1,000 in cash including $500 in profit…pay tax of approximately $100, and have $900 left to reinvest.

You would end up with your original $1,000 still invested in 50 shares and an additional $900 to reinvest in a new investment to diversify your portfolio.

---

Assets can also provide opportunities for reinvesting by producing new MAW dollars in the form of profits from income. This simply involves taking the income produced by an asset and using it to purchase an additional new investment asset. For example, I could take the dividends received from a stock, interest from a bond or the rent income from real estate and invest it to purchase more stock, bonds or real estate.

Whether form growth in market value or income, reinvesting profits builds wealth by multiplying the number of investment assets you own. Each new asset represents an additional opportunity to build wealth through growth in market value and/or income. Intelligent reinvesting allows you to keep your MAW dollars working at optimum wealth-building capacity.

Investing wisely requires an investment strategy suited to your objectives and resources—your goals and your supply of MAW dollars. To develop your strategy, you can start by asking yourself the same three basic questions you used in the SAVE pocket: How much?, How soon/How long? and Where?

## How Much?

Just as with the SAVE pocket, "How much?" is the first and most important question you must answer with your MAW dollars in the INVEST pocket...with one difference. In the INVEST pocket, "How much?" is a two-part question. The first question is, "How much do you have to invest?" The second question is, "How much do you need for a particular life goal?"

The answer to the first part will be a function of how successful you are at sustaining smart spending habits and maintaining an appropriate amount of savings. Remember that maintaining control over your money supply in the SPEND and SAVE pockets creates a continuous supply of MAW dollars in your INVEST pocket.

The answer to the second part will be a matter of estimating the amount of goald you will need to pay for various long-term life goals. Once you have established a goald objective, you can then analyze the growth potential and risk potential of various investments to find those best suited to your goal. The analysis will indicate how much you will need to invest in order to reach your goald target. Your research may lead you to selecting a single investment or multiple investments toward funding a particular goal.

The type of Money Person you are will also be a factor in your investment selections. Your tolerance of risk will be the dominant influence, both in terms of the amount you invest and the type of investment you choose. Because of the constant presence of risk, it is impossible to accurately predict the future value of an investment.

Passengers on the Money Ride who don't mind risk tend to prefer more aggressive investments. These are investments which offer the potential to either make a lot of money or lose a lot of money. They may also offer quick profits, as opposed to slow and steady long-term growth of MAW dollars.

On the other hand, passengers who aren't comfortable with risk prefer more conservative investments. These are investments where there is little risk of losing MAW dollars. They are usually less likely to make a lot of money or make it as quickly as aggressive, high-risk investments. At times, the conservative passenger may feel more comfortable keeping more MAW dollars in the SAVE pocket rather than in the INVEST pocket.

Since growth can be so unpredictable, perhaps the best answer to the "How much?" question is with "As much as possible." By stashing as many MAW dollars as possible in your INVEST pocket, you may be able to choose investments with less risk and still end up with enough or even more than enough goald to fund your life goals.

So, ultimately your success in the INVEST pocket will come down to how many MAW dollars you have to invest, how many MAW dollars you want to have for future goals and what kind of Money Person you are.

Finally, in order to maintain good INVEST money habits it is important to continue to regularly stash MAW dollars in your INVEST pocket. You can accomplish this by simply redirecting your budgeted MAW dollars to the INVEST pocket as soon as you have accumulated sufficient MAW dollars in your SAVE pocket. This way investing becomes a habit, just as saving should be.

Now, we cover the next INVEST pocket decision, "How soon/ How long."

## How Soon/How Long?

The INVEST pocket is typically used only for generating goald for long-term goals. These are goals which are more than four years into the future. This makes investing a matter of timing and profit.

The lifelong pursuit of building wealth can often be divided into timetables for particular life goals, such as major purchases, education funding and retirement.

The timetable of an investment is called its holding period—how long you plan to own the investment before hopefully selling it for a profit and converting it to cash. Ideally, the ultimate timetable of an investment will suit the timetable of a particular goal. This timing will rarely be perfect, but it is still sound planning to match the holding period in your investment choices with your goal timetables.

In addition to the goal timetables, the type of investment will also determine its holding period. Investments intended for growth in value will ultimately be converted to cash in order to fund goals and will have a limited holding period. Investments which generate income can be held for as long as the income generates a profit and is sufficient to meet the need for which it is intended.

Once you have invested the MAW dollars that will eventually fund a goal, you must monitor the investment's performance regularly—monthly, quarterly, annually—to keep the timetable of the investment and the goal in step.

Now that you are aware of the influence of timing on your INVEST pocket decisions, you're ready to deal with the final INVEST pocket question—"Where?"

## Where?

There are investment opportunities waiting for you at every twist and turn on the Money Ride. The number and variety of choices may seem overwhelming at times, but all investment opportunities will fall into one of five basic categories: business ownership, stocks and bonds, real estate, commodities and collectibles.

## Business Ownership

Business ownership means owning your own business, either by yourself or with one or more partners. Any company which is owned by a limited number of individuals where the ownership opportunity is not available to the general public is a "privately held" company.

The incentive for being a business owner is the opportunity to create wealth by growing the value of your business. The value of your business will be based upon its capacity to generate a profit by having more money coming in as income than you have money going out as expenses. The higher your profits, the higher the value of your business.

On the Money Ride, profitable businesses are called "right side up" businesses and unprofitable businesses are called "upside down" businesses.

In an ideal world, your business would be "right side up" all the time, but this is tough to accomplish. In fact, most businesses experience times when they are not generating profits, especially when they are first getting started.

In order to survive and prosper, the unprofitable times must be seldom and brief—on the Money Ride you don't want to get stuck "upside down." As long as your business is operating "right side up," you're earning an income and building wealth.

 **Passenger Tips & Tools #21**

### Want to Be an Entrepreneur?

Entrepreneurs play an important role in our society and economy. They are the people who are willing to risk everything they own to create a business, and if they are successful they reap the rewards they deserve.

So, if you want to be one, first go work for one and learn by first being a productive employee. Show initiative, ask questions, watch and learn…it's how many successful business owners start—as a hard-working, productive employee.

In addition to earning an income and building wealth, there are other benefits to owning your own business. As the owner of a company you get to work for yourself. You are your own boss.

As your own boss you have more freedom to do the work you want to do and work the way you want. But with the freedom also comes responsibility and risk—the responsibility of making all the key decisions and the risk of possibly losing everything you have invested in the business.

If you want to be a business owner on the Money Ride, prepare yourself for a special adventure. All the freedom, creativity, uncertainty, excitement and challenge of being a business owner make for a ride that can get wild and crazy at times!

Your first challenge as a business owner will be to decide what kind of products or services your company will sell. Ideally, it will offer products or services that people need or want.

Regardless of whether it offers a product or service, every business operates in its customers' SPEND pocket. As your customers buy your products or services, their SPEND dollars represent revenue to your business. Every revenue dollar you don't spend on the expenses of running your company is a dollar of profit.

As the owner, you can either take profit dollars as personal income or reinvest profit dollars to grow your business. As your business grows, if you manage it well its profits will continue to increase. As profits increase, the value of your business increases—this is how a business owner creates wealth.

When you have succeeded at building a profitable business, you will find yourself with three options: (1) maintain your full participation and ownership; (2) reduce your ownership and/or participation by selling a portion of your interest in the business; (3) sell your entire interest in your company.

In addition to the financial rewards of building a successful business, there is the personal satisfaction that comes from adding value to the lives of your employees, your customers and your community.

## Stocks

Stocks and bonds are the most popular investments for employing the accumulation approach to building wealth. However, stocks and bonds are different in what they do and how they do it.

A stock represents a fractional share of ownership in a company organized as a corporation. Corporations can be private or public companies.

Private companies are corporations which usually have a small number of shareholders; the shares are bought and sold privately among individuals. Private corporations are also called "privately-held companies."

Public companies are corporations which usually have large numbers of shares owned by the investing public. Their shares are typically bought and sold on public markets called securities exchanges. Buy-and-sell stock trades are transacted through financial companies known as securities dealers. Investment firms, banks, insurance companies and financial planning firms typically have a relationship with a securities dealer so that their representatives can sell stocks and other investments to the public.

When you own a company's stock, you own a proportional share of the company's value, defined by the market price of a share. As a shareholder, you often have the right to vote on decisions about how the company is run. You also share in the profits and losses of the company. When the share price goes up the value of your investment goes up, and when the share price drops your investment loses value.

The degree of change from up to down in a stock's price is called volatility. A stock whose price changes dramatically from high to low is said to be volatile. Regardless of the degree of volatility, these increases and decreases in price and value are how you make or lose your MAW dollars investing in stocks.

In addition to increasing share price, stocks can contribute to wealth-building a second way. Some companies distribute a portion of profits to the shareholders in cash payments called dividends. Dividends are typically paid annually or quarterly. As a shareholder you have the option to either take the dividend as cash or use it to buy more fractional shares in the company for future growth.

Regardless of whether you invest in stocks for growth or income, you need to have an organized approach to selecting stocks. A selection of stocks is called a stock portfolio and should contain a variety of different types of companies with different growth and risk potential. Having a variety of stocks in a portfolio is called diversification. Diversification helps to increase the opportunity for growth and spread the exposure to risk.

Stocks can be grouped into three classes, based on company size: large capital, medium capital and small capital. The "capital" stands for the amount of money a company has. Size is important because it is related to the growth and risk potential of a company.

Small companies typically offer the greatest growth upside and risk downside. Small companies have a lot of potential to grow, but they also represent significant risk because they have less capital to weather hard times and stay competitive. This means that you can expect the share price of your small company stocks to experience greater price fluctuation than the shares of larger companies—greater price volatility. Your small company stocks will definitely add some excitement to your Money Ride adventure.

Medium-size companies offer a more moderate degree of growth and risk potential than smaller companies. They may also offer the potential for dividend income. The shares you own in medium-size companies are the middle ground of your diversified portfolio. They offer less risk potential than small company stocks, along with greater growth potential than large company stocks.

Large companies offer less potential for immediate growth, less risk and greater long-term stability than small- and medium-size companies. They also offer more potential for dividend income. Your large company stocks will serve as the stable, long-term foundation of your portfolio.

## Bonds

Bonds are different from stocks, both in how they work and in the role they play in your INVEST pocket. Bonds are generally considered to have less risk than stocks and are used primarily for safety and income.

---

 **Passenger Tips & Tools #22**

### Loaner vs. Owner

Remember that you do not invest in bonds for growth. With bonds you are a "loaner" not an "owner." When a bond matures, your original principal is returned to you…before the maturity date you only receive simple interest on your principal, no real growth.

Bonds have an important role in an investment portfolio, but safety and income is what they are used for, not growth.

---

When corporations and government entities need additional capital for general use or specific projects, they raise the money by issuing bonds which they sell to the public. Owning a bond is like owning an IOU for the money you lend to the issuing entity.

A bond is a promise by the issuing entity to repay the amount borrowed and to pay the bond holder interest for the use of the money. The interest payments are typically paid to the bond holder every six months.

The promise to repay is backed either by the financial strength of the issuing entity or by the income generated by the specific use of the bond proceeds, such as building toll roads and bridges. This financial backing is the bondholder's assurance that the interest will be paid and the debt repaid. If the issuing entity is unable to pay interest or repay the debt, the bondholder has a right to receive repayment from the financial assets of the entity. This financial backing is what gives a bond an added degree of safety over other investments.

A bond works much like a CD except that the term of a bond is longer and the interest paid is usually higher. The term of a bond typically ranges from one to thirty years, depending upon whether the bond issuer is a company or government entity.

The beginning of the bond term is called the "issue date" and the end of the bond term is called the "maturity date." The bondholder receives interest payments during the bond term based on the bond's fixed interest rate, called the "coupon rate." For bonds with a term longer than one year, the interest payments are typically made every six months. A bond must be repaid no later than its maturity date. However, a bond may be repaid sooner by the issuing entity if the bond agreement allows.

The interest paid on bonds issued by corporations and the federal government is taxed just like your paycheck, as ordinary income. However, interest paid on bonds issued by city, county and state governments is federal tax-free and state tax-free if you live in the state in which the bond is issued.

Normally, a bond's longer term would suggest less liquidity, but this is not necessarily the case. Like stocks, bonds are bought and sold in the financial markets through securities firms. This gives them a measure of liquidity in spite of their longer term.

A bond's price moves up and down with the prevailing market interest rates. When the prevailing market interest rate rises above a bond's coupon rate, the bond's price drops. When the prevailing market interest drops below the coupon rate, the bond's price rises. You can sell a bond at any time prior to the maturity date to either raise cash or earn a profit by selling at a higher price.

If you hold a bond until its maturity date, the loan is repaid and you get your original investment back. This means that you received interest income during the bond term, but you do not realize any growth on your investment.

So, if you purchase a stock you are an "owner" and if you purchase a bond you are a "loaner." Owners take more risks and are ultimately concerned with a "return on their principal." Loaners, on the other hand, take little or no risk in return for a stable income flow and are ultimately more concerned with the "return of their principal."

Now that you know the basics of investing in individual stocks and bonds, it's a good time to learn about an alternative way to build a stock and bond portfolio—mutual funds.

## Mutual Funds

Mutual funds are the most popular way to invest in stocks and bonds. You will find that over half of the passengers you meet on the Money Ride invest in mutual funds.

It is important to understand that mutual funds are not a separate type of investment like stocks, bonds and real estate, they are instead what is called an "investment structure." They are a method of packaging an investment product for sale to the public. The package is the mutual fund, and the contents are usually portfolios of stocks and/or bonds.

There are two basic advantages to using mutual funds in your INVEST pocket—diversification and professional management.

Mutual funds operate on the basic principle of diversification. A mutual fund is an investment company which collects MAW dollars from the public and invests the pool of money in stocks and/or bonds. The large pool of money enables the investment company to purchase thousands of shares of hundreds of companies, creating a much larger portfolio than you can as an individual. This allows you to participate in a well-diversified portfolio which spreads risk and expands the opportunity for growth.

Mutual funds employ investment experts who create and manage a large portfolio of individual stocks and bonds on your behalf. The investment management team makes buy-and-sell decisions for you, taking the guesswork out of your stock and bond investment choices.

The mutual fund charges a fee for managing the fund's portfolio. The fee is based on a percentage of the fund's total value and is deducted periodically from the fund's earnings or assets.

When you invest in a mutual fund, you purchase shares in the fund rather than shares of individual stocks or bonds. The shares of mutual funds are not publicly traded like individual shares of stocks and bonds. The shares of mutual funds are offered and redeemed by a company authorized as the fund's distributor.

Every mutual fund has a particular investment objective, which can be defined by the kind of stocks and bonds it owns or by its investment style. The terms "large cap," "international" and "S&P 500 index" are examples of mutual funds defined by what they own. The terms "growth," "value" and "aggressive growth" are examples of mutual funds defined by their management style.

Mutual funds take the guesswork out of picking individual stocks and bonds, but you will still have some homework to do in choosing a mutual fund. You will have over 8,000 mutual funds to choose from on the Money Ride, and you must base your choices on the funds' objectives, investment styles, management fees and long-term performance record.

 **Passenger Tips & Tools #23**

### Picking a Mutual Fund

Don't chase short-term performance records…look for a fund with a leading long-term performance history.

Look for fund managers who have been with a fund for a long time.

Compare fund expenses and fees…both decrease a fund's gains.

Match the fund's investment objective and risk/reward potential with your investment objectives and risk tolerance.

## Real Estate

Real estate is usually a long-term investment, which offers the potential for income and growth. Real estate generates income by charging people rent to use the property. The growth comes from the increase in the market price of a property.

The income and growth potential of real estate is primarily determined by its location. Depending upon its intended use, you want to invest in a property that is located where people want to live or work. The current and future economic prospects for the area are also an important consideration.

There are three basic types of real estate. The first type is land, which is property that does not have any buildings on it. The second type is residential real estate, which is property with buildings where people live. The third type is commercial real estate, which is land with buildings where people work.

When investing in land, the goal is either to hold the land for resale or to build something on it. Holding it for resale usually means owning a property for a longer period of time. The hope is that eventually the property's location will attract a buyer who is willing to pay a higher price than what you paid for it.

Land can also be purchased with the plan to build a residential or commercial building on the property. The process of buying land and then constructing a building on it is called "developing" and people who do it are called "developers."

As a developer, your goal is to ultimately sell a property for much more than the combined cost of the land and the building construction. Instead of selling the developed property, you may choose to keep it for its rental income and growth potential.

The more common INVEST pocket opportunity in real estate is to buy an existing residential or commercial property. With an existing property, the initial goal is generate sufficient rental income to pay expenses and generate a profit in the form of positive cash flow. This is not always possible to achieve when you first buy a property, but achieving profitability as soon as possible will be the goal with every real estate investment.

Regardless of the type of property you decide to buy on the Money Ride, real estate has an advantage over other investments in how it's purchased—OPM.

## OPM

When you buy real estate, the money you pay for it does not all have to be yours. You actually get to use "other peoples' money"—

OPM—to pay part of the purchase price of a property. The other great thing about it is that your part of the total money needed can be a lot smaller than the OPM part. So, where does the OPM come from?

You get OPM from banks. OPM is the money people deposit in the banks as savings. Banks take part of their depositors' money and loan it to people so that they can buy real estate. The bank will loan you as much as 80% or more of the purchase price of the property you want to buy. This purchase loan arrangement with a bank is called "financing."

This means you pay 20% of the purchase price and the bank loans you the money to pay the other 80%. You then use the rent income you collect from the property to make loan payments to the bank. The loan payments include repaying the loan, plus an interest charge for the use of the OPM.

Over time, your loan payments will pay off the loan and you will own 100% of the property. In the meantime, you get the rents you collect. Plus, any growth in the value of the real estate increases the value of your investment. As good as this sounds, it is not the best part—keep reading.

When it comes to reinvesting, real estate has a unique advantage over the other types of investments. With most investments, in order to reinvest cash from profits, you must first pay tax on the profits when you sell the investment.

With real estate you can actually take cash profits out of a property without having to sell the property. You also don't have to pay tax on the profit until you ultimately sell the property. This is accomplished by using a strategy called refinancing.

Refinancing is a method of replacing the loan (mortgage) originally used to purchase the property a new loan. The strategy allows you to convert the difference between the original and current value to new MAW cash for reinvesting without paying tax at the time of the transaction. The cash can then be used to purchase a new property to expand a real estate portfolio.

The opportunity to use refinancing take profits without paying current taxes, gives real estate a special advantage when it comes to reinvesting.

---

 **Passenger Tips & Tools #24**

### The Real Estate Advantage

Franklin Frugal and Freddy Flash together purchased a rental house in 1997 for $100,000 using a cash down payment of $20,000 and a mortgage loan from a bank of $80,000.

In 2007 the market value of the property had grown to $180,000 and the amount still owed on the mortgage was $65,000. Franklin and Freddy decided they wanted to use some of the increased value of the property to buy another house for $180,000 to expand their real estate empire...refinancing was the answer and here is how it worked.

They figured that they needed about $36,000 for a down payment and a mortgage loan of $144,000 to buy the new property. So, the refinance of the original property would consist of a new mortgage of $101,000 to pay off the existing mortgage of $65,000 and leave $36,000 in cash (new MAW dollars) for the cash down payment to purchase the new property.

Franklin and Freddy now own two houses worth a total of $360,000 with total mortgage debt of $245,000 for a net equity value of $115,000...all created by an initial cash investment of $20,000 on the first house.

---

Keep in mind that the values, prices, interest rates and percentage of OPM will change, depending on the economy. However, the basic approach to building wealth in real estate is real and always available in your INVEST pocket when the right opportunity presents itself.

Though there are only five basic categories of investments in your INVEST pocket, remember that there are an infinite number of variations on the opportunities across the three categories to chose from.

So, while you're roaring along on your Money Ride adventure

keep your eyes and ears open and your imagination alert to the abundant opportunities that await you at every twist, turn, peak and valley.

Read quickly now—two last pockets to learn about before your Money Ride adventure begins.

 **Passenger Watch**

Franklin and Sonya are both feeling pretty good about their recent INVEST pocket decisions. Two of the stocks Sonya has owned for a few years have begun to show promising results. Franklin started a new business with two partners, and they are already profitable thanks to Franklin's frugal grip on the company's cash flow.

Suzie's INVEST pocket is empty, but she has new furniture! Suzie's spending is leading down the path to financial disaster, but she has new furniture!

Freddy is actually doing okay with his INVEST pocket ventures. He does know quality and was smart enough to do his risk/reward homework to make some good stock choices.

# 8. The Protect Pocket

## Expect the Unexpected

There are plenty of potential bumps, bruises and accidents lurking around every corner on the Money Ride—if you're not prepared, they can cost you.

That's why the PROTECT pocket can be the most important pocket on your vest. It's the pocket that "has your back"…that "has you covered." It's the pocket that assures that everything you are trying to achieve financially on the Money Ride won't be derailed by some unexpected loss.

Regardless of the type of loss you may face, protection against the risk of it happening will play an important role in your financial success on the Money Ride. Many of the money decisions you make will involve elements that you can control, but risk is not one of them. You cannot control unexpected events, but you can protect yourself against the risk of financial loss, should the unexpected happen.

Protection against the risk of unexpected loss is called "insurance," but it really should be called "assurance" because that's what it really provides—the assurance that the wealth-building flow of MAW dollars throughout the pockets on your Opportunity Vest will continue, no matter what unexpected things might happen in your life.

The idea of assurance is important because a loss suffered can generate a negative financial domino effect throughout the other four vest pockets. Any loss may cause either a direct outflow of SPEND pocket dollars or the ripple effect of having to use SAVE pocket, INVEST pocket—or worse yet—BORROW pocket dollars to cover the loss.

This domino effect can be as minor as a small additional expense in the SPEND pocket or as serious as entirely stopping the flow of PAW dollars to your vest. Regardless of the degree of loss, an unprotected loss essentially steals MAW dollars from the vest pockets and disrupts the wealth building process.

## Health, Income, Property & Life

The four financial domains of potential loss are your health, income, property and life.

### Loss of Health

If you have to see a doctor, visit a clinic or go to a hospital because you are sick or injured, you will be charged for any treatment and medicine you receive.

Health insurance is designed to protect you from exposure to medical costs. You will be able to purchase health insurance either under an individual health policy or a group health policy.

You purchase individual coverage personally and pay the entire cost yourself. You can cover yourself as well as your immediate family members under an individual policy.

Group coverage may be available to you if you are a member of a group of people such as employees of a company or a professional association. Group health coverage is purchased through the group, and you typically will only pay a portion of the total coverage cost.

### Loss of Income

Except for simply losing your job, income loss is usually caused by an illness or injury. If you are too sick or injured to work, your flow of PAW dollars stops.

Disability income insurance is a form of health insurance that is designed to replace a portion of your income if you are unable to work due to an injury or illness.

This coverage pays a monthly benefit equal to a percentage of your total monthly income, up to a maximum of approximately 66%. The benefit is paid for a stipulated period of time, which varies depending on the type of policy.

Like standard health insurance, you can buy disability insurance using either an individual disability policy or a group disability policy, depending on your situation.

## Loss of Property

If any of your personal property, real estate, cars or other assets are damaged or lost, there will be a cost to fix or replace the affected property.

Property and casualty insurance is the type of protection you will need as you accumulate assets on the Money Ride. This type of protection pays the cost to replace or repair property such as cars, homes, furnishings and other valuable assets.

This type of insurance may also offer a special type of protection called personal liability insurance. It is usually offered as part of the coverage on auto and real property insurance policies. Personal liability coverage protects you in the event you accidentally cause a loss or damage to someone's property. It is especially important protection to have as part of your auto insurance—there are some crazy drivers on the Money Ride.

## Loss of Life

When you die, anyone who relies on you financially will lose the income you shared with them or used to support them.

This generally includes family members, but can also include business partners who rely on your contributions to the profitability of the company. It's also advisable to have sufficient life insurance protection to pay off any debts you owe.

Regardless of what type of insurance is involved, in the PROTECT pocket, your decisions will be guided by three basic principles: risk transfer, cost sharing and full replacement value.

## Risk Transfer

It is a good idea to transfer risk away from yourself whenever possible. This is what insurance does—you pay the insurance company to assume risk.

Insurance protects your PAW and MAW dollars from the cost of a loss as you rumble along on your Money Ride adventure. For the protection, you will pay the insurance company a fee called a "premium."

Insurance premiums are a fixed expense in your SPEND pocket budget. You can pay insurance premiums annually, semi-annually, quarterly or monthly.

Even if you decide not to buy insurance to transfer a risk, you are still insured, but now you are the insurance company and assume all the risk of loss yourself. It's called being "self-insured." When you are self-insured, you are essentially betting that a certain event is not going to happen.

If you want to be self-insured for any potential loss, you better have a lot of PAW and MAW dollars stashed in your Opportunity Vest. However, if the potential financial loss tied to the event is too great, you may want to reconsider self-insurance and transfer the risk away from yourself…using an insurance company.

## Cost Sharing

It is important to know that even if you purchase protection against a potential loss, you won't always be able to transfer 100% of the risk. Depending on the type of coverage you buy, you may have to pay some portion of the cost to repair or replace the affected asset. On the Money Ride, this is called "cost sharing."

The cost sharing portion you pay under the terms of an insurance policy are typically referred to as the "deductible" and may also include "co-pay" or "out-of-pocket" expenses. If a loss occurs, you pay your portion of the cost and the insurance company pays the rest. So, the portion you pay is essentially self-insurance.

**Passenger Tips & Tools #25**

**Deductibles & Reserves**

Deductibles are an important tool in controlling the cost of insurance. It is, however, important that you always have sufficient MAW dollars in your SAVE pocket to cover your deductible exposure. So, when you figure your fixed MAW contribution expense in your monthly budget, be sure to factor in the amount of your deductibles.

Depending upon the type of insurance, you usually have a choice as to the amount of the deductible. The higher the deductible, the more you will pay if a loss occurs. A higher deductible also means that it will cost you less to purchase the insurance because you assume more of the risk.

In the PROTECT pocket, the total potential cost for any insurance is the premiums you pay plus the deductible amount you must pay in the event of a loss. This makes cost sharing an important tool for balancing protection needs with protection costs.

## Full Replacement Value

The amount of protection purchased to cover any potential loss should be equal to the cost to entirely restore or replace an affected asset. On the Money Ride, this is called full replacement value (FRV).

In some cases, FRV may be the money needed to pay expenses resulting from a loss. In other cases it may be the amount of money needed to replace lost income or repair/replace lost property.

FRV is important because if the amount of protection is not sufficient to cover the cost of the loss, then you may have to use MAW dollars or, worse, borrow money to make up the difference. In this way, FRV protects all of your assets, not just the asset directly affected by a loss.

It is important to use FRV to determine the appropriate amount of protection, because it assures that the wealth-building process throughout your Opportunity Vest can continue if an unexpected loss occurs.

---

**Passenger Tips & Tools #26**

### FRV & Old Stuff

It is often not cost-effective and sometimes not possible to insure older assets or property for full replacement cost.

If the annual premium cost is greater than the FRV or if the insurable benefit is less than the FRV, it may be time to realize that the property's sentimental value is all you have left and insurance is not an economical option.

---

Remember that the risk of unexpected loss is lurking in the shadows at every twist and turn along the Money Ride. But do not fear, because armed with the tools of risk transfer, cost sharing and full replacement value, you'll be able to design your own custom-fitted insurance suit of armor to protect you.

Time is growing short—your ride is about to begin. One last pocket left to explore, but it is just as important as the others, so read carefully.

On to the BORROW pocket!

## 🐜 Passenger Watch

Freddy had a mishap in his new sports car. The car damage is covered, but Freddy is going to be laid up for a while—no work, no income, no disability insurance. He will have to liquidate some of his investments or borrow money to get by until he recovers.

Franklin's company office was damaged by a recent storm. No problem, Franklin made sure when he took over managing the company finances that they had the right kind and right amount of property coverage.

Suzie is shopping for health coverage which is not the kind of shopping she is good at. She's smart enough to know when she is out of her element and has asked Franklin for suggestions.

Sonya has no insurance issues. She has all of her property covered for FRV and has her income and life insured as well. Because she has plenty of MAW dollars in savings and investments, she is able to take advantage of deductibles to keep her premiums low.

# 9. The Borrow Pocket

## Borrowing: From D² to −S²

This is the pocket where you find the money you need to make purchases or investments for which you don't have the cash in your SPEND, SAVE or INVEST pockets. The BORROW pocket on your Opportunity Vest contributes to your efforts to build wealth and enjoy life through smart borrowing decisions.

You probably noticed that the BORROW pocket is so large that it nearly covers the entire back of your Opportunity Vest. It's big because the money decisions you make in this pocket can make a *big* difference in your financial life. This is the pocket where you will have lots of opportunities to succeed and fail, based upon your understanding of what borrowing can do *for* you and what it can do *to* you.

---

 **Passenger Tips & Tools #27**

### Whom Do You Work For?

Having too much debt is like having a second job that doesn't pay you…you pay it.

Some people simultaneously have multiple jobs that cost them instead of paying them. In addition to their regular job, they work for a bank, an auto finance company and one or more credit card companies.

Whom do you work for?

---

In the BORROW pocket, the difference between "for you" and "to you" involves a familiar dynamic you learned about in the SPEND pocket: D²—discretion and discipline.

Passengers who exercise $D^2$ are able to make sensible use of their BORROW pocket as a form of $+S^2$ (smart spending) and enjoy an abundant, happy life on the Money Ride.

Passengers who do not exercise $D^2$ end up using their BORROW pocket as a form of $-S^2$ (stupid spending). As a result, they experience a long, tough, bumpy ride and often find themselves stuck in the Chasm of Financial Despair.

In order to make smart borrowing decisions, you need to remember the three key dynamics of the BORROW pocket:

1. OPM mechanics
2. Your borrowing score
3. Good debt vs. bad debt

## OPM Mechanics

You learned a little about OPM (other peoples' money) in the INVEST pocket discussion of real estate. There are many other uses of OPM beyond real estate, which are available in the BORROW pocket. Because of its many potential uses, it's important to understand the mechanics of OPM.

In the BORROW pocket, your sources of OPM may include individuals and financial institutions such as banks, credit unions or credit card companies.

You only get to use OPM dollars temporarily, and then you must pay them back. This temporary use is called a loan, and all loans are also generally called "debt." A loan is a legal agreement (contract) between two parties to borrow OPM. You are the "borrower" and the source of the OPM dollars is the "lender." The money you borrow is called the "principal" and the fee you pay to borrow the money is called "interest." The unpaid portion of a loan is called the "outstanding balance," and when a loan is entirely repaid it's said to be "paid off." If you are late making a payment you are "delinquent." If you fail to repay a loan you are considered to be in "default" and as far as the lender is concerned, the fault is yours.

Every loan agreement has specific rules governing your use

of the money as the borrower. The rules generally cover four main points:

## 1. How much money you may borrow (loan amount)

The principal amount you are able to borrow will be a function of two factors: your borrowing score and collateral. We will talk about your borrowing score in a minute. First, a brief word about collateral. Collateral can be your income or property you own that the lender has the legal right to take if you don't repay the loan. Most of the time, the property you purchase with the loan is the collateral, such as cars or houses. Other times, you may have to pledge other property as collateral or show proof of sufficient income in order to get a loan.

## 2. How much you must pay to borrow the money (interest rate and loan fees)

In addition to paying back the principal amount of the loan, you will also have to pay interest. The interest you pay will be based on an annual percentage rate (5%, 6.5% etc.) and each loan payment will include a fraction of the annual interest fee. In addition to the interest charge, there may also be additional fees you have to pay to secure a loan. These are generally referred to as "finance charges" or "loan fees."

## 3. How much time you have to pay back the loan and the amount of the payments (repayment terms)

Every loan has a repayment schedule which describes the duration of the loan, the frequency of payments and the total number of payments. The payment schedule will tell you exactly the portion of each payment that goes toward repaying the principal and the portion that goes toward paying the interest charge.

## 4. How you must meet other requirements or conditions of the loan (performance conditions)

Every loan agreement has rules, requirements and conditions which the borrower must satisfy. Penalties for violating the rules can range from paying extra fees and higher interest rates to canceling the loan and requiring early repayment of the outstanding balance.

There are laws governing lending which require certain duties of both the lender and the borrower. Even before the law, common sense suggests that as a borrower you have a special duty to yourself to know exactly what you are in for when you borrow money—know your duties and know your rights.

So, the first rule of smart borrowing is "know the rules" of borrowing before you borrow.

---

 **Passenger Tips & Tools #28**

### Read Before You "Sign Here"

Anyone of majority age can execute a contract and be legally bound by its terms. Know your OPM mechanics and legal obligations, and ask questions before you sign.

---

## Good Debt & Bad Debt

There are many types of loans available for you to choose from on the Money Ride as you race along. This means your BORROW pocket choices can be tempting, confusing and fast-paced. To keep it simple, remember that all loans represent one of two basic forms of debt—good debt and bad debt.

## Good Debt

All good debt has two fundamental characteristics: affordable payments and economic advantage.

Affordable payments are payments which fit easily within your monthly budget. This means that the payments do not force you to make drastic changes in your SPEND, SAVE and INVEST pockets, which could compromise your basic lifestyle or cause you to sacrifice important financial goals and opportunities.

**Passenger Tips & Tools #29**

### Cap Your Debt

A good rule for managing debt is to limit your *total* monthly debt payments to an amount not greater than 20% of your take-home income.

Nowhere on your Opportunity Vest is the domino effect between pockets more apparent than with the decisions you will make in your BORROW pocket. Be careful that the first falling domino of your borrowing decision does not distract you from the other displaced dominos and their impact on your other vest pockets.

Because your money supply is finite, good debt decisions will require $D^2$. Securing affordable payments should be a top priority with every borrowing decision. This practice will help keep your borrowing score high by keeping debt low and making it easier to make payments on time.

The second good debt characteristic is "economic advantage." This means that good debt either helps you affordably meet important needs and goals or helps you build wealth by acquiring assets.

There may be times when financial emergencies require more money than your PAW income or MAW dollars in reserve can cover. Your ability to borrow the necessary funds to keep your financial stability intact can be considered good debt. An education loan used to earn a degree or learn a new skill in order to earn more income can also be considered good debt. A car loan could likewise be considered good debt if the car is required for earning a living.

Good debt is also valuable in funding various opportunities in your INVEST pocket to build wealth. It could be for real estate or for a business. Whether it is real estate, a business or some other type of investment, good debt is an excellent way to use OPM to create additional income and growth.

There will be all kinds of opportunities for using good debt on the Money Ride—so stay alert!

## Bad Debt

No fun—that's what bad debt is on the Money Ride. So, where does it come from and how can you avoid it?

Bad debt is simply any loan that you can't afford. It comes from a lack of $D^2$ in borrowing decisions, which most often involve the SPEND pocket. This SPEND pocket bad debt is created by simply spending money you don't have. This is accomplished by using OPM to buy things that you don't have the cash to purchase. It may be the payments you can't afford or the total repayment or both—either way you lose because you simply have too much debt.

Credit cards are what most Money Ride passengers use to get themselves in a jam with bad debt. It usually happens with two critical missteps. First, they use credit card OPM to spend cash they don't have.

Second, they fail to pay off the outstanding balance each month. This means that they then have to pay monthly interest on the amount owed until it is paid off. This can in turn lead to the worst situation where if the borrower cannot make the required payments and defaults on a loan.

Credit cards are not the only way to get yourself into trouble with bad debt. Any source of OPM which you use to buy stuff you can't afford will have the same *no fun* impact on your Money Ride

 **Passenger Tips & Tools #30**

### Hello...Anyone Home?

Having to pay credit card interest on something you buy means paying more for the item than if you simply used cash. This is a really good example of $-S^2$, stupid spending. It is also a good example of what is known on the Money Ride as self-inflicted inflation.

adventure. It doesn't matter where the OPM comes from or how necessary the item is, any debt you can't afford is bad debt.

On the Money Ride, bad debt is no fun because it takes too many dollars away from opportunities to enjoy life today and tomorrow.

Every dollar of bad debt in your BORROW pocket is wrapped around a heavy brick. The more bad debt you have, the heavier the weight you have to carry on your back.

You will see some passengers on the Money Ride who are so weighed down with bad debt that they can hardly move. They lose the flexibility needed to keep reaching for Grabbing Dollars. This means that there will be fewer MAW dollars available to take advantage of wealth-building opportunities throughout the pockets on your Opportunity Vest.

Remember that bad debt is like stealing money from yourself, because it eliminates opportunity. The more bad debt you accumulate, the less wealth you'll end up with.

Your ability to make sensible use of debt will enable you to take advantage of good debt opportunities to affordably acquire assets and grow wealth. It will also help you avoid bad debt and all of its limiting and decaying effects on your cash flow and wealth.

## Your Borrowing Score

The amount of OPM dollars you will have available to you will depend upon how sensible you are with your borrowing. Lenders keep track of your borrowing behavior to determine how much OPM money you get to use and on what terms you get to use it.

There are special companies that keep track of borrowing data on you and every other Money Ride passenger. The companies then create a credit report which profiles each individual's borrowing activity. Your borrowing score, known as your "credit score," is based on the information in your credit report.

Your borrowing score is called your FICO score. Your FICO score tells a lender how well it can financially rely on your ability to make payments on time and to pay off a loan, including interest and fees.

Your FICO score is like your OPM qualifying exam, and your performance on the exam shows how good of a repayment risk you are. Unlike the exams you take in school, your FICO exam goes on forever. Every time you borrow money for anything, that borrowing event can have an impact on your FICO score.

If your FICO score is high, you are considered a good risk to a lender. If it is low, you're a bad risk. If you want to score high on your FICO exam, keep your debt low in relation to your income, always make payments on time and limit the number of credit accounts in your name.

Money Ride passengers with high FICO scores always have more OPM dollars available than those with low scores. Those with

 **Passenger Tips & Tools #31**

### Your Borrowing Score

The highest FICO score possible is 850 and the lowest is 300. Anything above 720 is generally considered to be in the top tier. So, keep your score in the mid to high 700s and you'll be able to readily access OPM when you need it.

low FICO scores typically are allowed to borrow less OPM and have to pay higher interest rates to borrow it. Some passengers have a FICO score so low that they cannot borrow any OPM.

So, to make the most of OPM opportunities in your BOR-ROW pocket, pay attention to your borrowing habits and keep your FICO score high.

---

### 🐎 Passenger Watch

Poor Suzie has so many bricks in her BORROW pocket that she can barely move. Fortunately she has two college degrees so that she gets a big net to grab PAW dollars. Sadly, she can't possibly fulfill her grabbing potential with all the bad debt holding her down. In addition to her regular job, Suzie now also works for three credit card companies and two banks—paying them over 60% of what she earns at her regular job.

Franklin is on schedule to pay off his house and retire by age 50. He has no other debt.

Sonya is in no hurry to pay off her house; she would rather have the money in her investment portfolio where it will grow faster than her home's value. Her debt payments each month are less that 20% of her take-home pay.

Freddy has realized that his house payment is just too much; it's taking all his fun money to cover it. He plans on finding a smaller place, but he won't leave his exclusive neighborhood—after all, he does have his image to maintain!

# 10. Time to Buckle Up!

That's it! You now have all the basic information you'll need to make the most of your Money Ride adventure.

Keep this guide close at hand! It will be your handy reference for making the most of the opportunities and challenges waiting for you on the Money Ride.

The time has come! Hurry inside now. Jump into the first empty car you see and buckle up! Get loose and be ready to start grabbing and vesting your lifetime share of Money Ride dollars.

Work hard, work smart, have fun, stay positive and always be alert for opportunities. Be aware of the Money Person you are, and learn from your own and your fellow passengers' Money Ride experiences.

Welcome to the Money Ride—it's the ride of a lifetime, and we are all on it!

## Glossary of Money Ride Terms

**Bad Debt** Any debt that is unaffordable in terms of the payments and/or the repayment.

**Borrowing Score** Also known as FICO score. Scoring system used to determine a person's credit worthiness based upon their borrowing activity.

**Chasm of Financial Despair** The chasm separating PAW and MAW representing the unhappiness caused by the failure to spend less than one earns.

**Compounding** The accumulation of money created by the continual crediting of interest on principal plus the interest earned in the prior periods.

**Cost Sharing** Splitting the cost of a loss between an insured and an insurance company. Typically achieved using deductibles, co-pays and out-of-pocket expenses.

**Domino Effect** The positive or negative effect of one dollar transaction on the other dollars in the money supply.

**Financing** Borrowing money either to purchase goods and services or to acquire assets.

**Fixed Expenses** Expenses which reoccur for the same amount each month.

**Full Replacement Value** Value of asset/property based upon the full cost to repair or replace asset/property

**Goald** MAW dollars designated for life goals.

**Good Debt** Debt which is affordable and which creates a financial advantage.

**MAW** Money at Work. Excess earnings invested to generated growth and/or income as part of the wealth-building process.

**Money Dynamics** The rules and mechanics of money which govern the efficient use of money.

**Money I.Q.** Knowledge and understanding of how money works and the ability to successfully apply that knowledge to a lifetime of money choices and decisions.

**Money Person** Personality type described in terms of behavior regarding money.

**OPM** Other Peoples' Money, the depositors' money a bank uses to make loans to its customers.

**PAW** People at Work, generating income by direct labor, a job, work etc.

**Risk Tolerance** A person's capacity to emotionally and financially assume the risk of loss.

**Risk Transfer** Transferring the risk of loss away from an individual to an insurance company by purchasing an insurance policy.

**Staging** Coordinating the liquidity timeline of various savings vehicles with the timeline of the proposed uses for the money.

**Today Dollars** PAW and MAW dollars which are needed for current expenses and/or investment.

**Tomorrow Dollars** MAW dollars in the SAVE and INVEST pockets designated for future uses.

**Variable Expenses** Monthly expenses for needs or wants which vary from month to month.

**Vest Dynamics** The mechanics of money affecting the flow of dollars throughout the pockets on the Opportunity Vest.

**Vested Dollars** Dollars which are positioned in the various pockets of the Opportunity Vest.

**Vesting** The process of stashing dollars in the various pockets of the Opportunity Vest.

**Wealth Bridge** Bridge created by a budget which spans the Chasm of Financial Despair.

**Work I.Q.** All of the education, job skills and personal skills you acquire that enable you to earn an income.

## Money Ride Formulas

These formulas and acronyms were created to serve as reminders to help passengers establish and sustain sound money habits.

**WORK I.Q. = INCOME • MONEY I.Q. = WEALTH**

---

**PAW & MAW • MONEY = COMMODITY**

---

**$SCARCITY$ • BUDGET= $D^2$ • $-S^2$ • $+S^2$**

---

**INFLATION / TAXES / SPENDING / MARKETS**

---

**SAVE = SAFE • FV = P $(1+i)^n$**

---

**INVEST = RISK/REWARD/GROWTH/INCOME**

---

**INVEST/DIVERSIFY/REINVEST**

---

**\<PROTECT \>**
**HEALTH/INCOME/PROPERTY/LIFE**

---

**GOOD DEBT vs. BAD DEBT • OPM • FICO**

## About the Author

William K. Busch is a financial advisor, educator and public speaker.

Bill has spent the past 27 years helping clients make smart money decisions to address a variety of financial issues and concerns.

He has utilized the diversity of his professional expertise and his background as a business educator to present workshops on personal finance for high school and college students.

This book is the culmination of his professional experiences working with clients and his years of developing techniques in the classroom for teaching the fundamentals of money and wealth.

Bill lives in La Jolla, California.

# NOTES

# NOTES

## NOTES

# 𝗧𝗠𝗥 The Money Ride

For more information on *The Money Ride*,
and to order additional copies of this book,
please visit

## www.moneyride.com